IN SEARCH OF
RETIREMENT SECURITY

IN SEARCH OF RETIREMENT SECURITY

THE CHANGING MIX OF SOCIAL INSURANCE, EMPLOYEE BENEFITS, AND INDIVIDUAL RESPONSIBILITY

EDITED BY
Teresa Ghilarducci, Van Doorn Ooms,
John L. Palmer, and Catherine Hill

A CENTURY FOUNDATION BOOK
COSPONSORED BY THE
NATIONAL ACADEMY OF SOCIAL INSURANCE

The Century Foundation Press • New York

The Century Foundation sponsors and supervises timely analyses of economic policy, foreign affairs, and domestic political issues. Not-for-profit and nonpartisan, it was founded in 1919 and endowed by Edward A. Filene.

LIBRARY OF CONGRESS CATALOGING-IN-PUBLICATION DATA

In search of retirement security : the changing mix of social insurance, employee benefits, and individual responsibility / edited by Teresa Ghilarducci . . . [et al.].
    p. cm.
  Based on papers delivered at the National Academy of Social Insurance's 16th annual conference, held January 22–23, 2004, at the National Press Club in Washington, D.C.
  Includes bibliographical references and index.
  ISBN 0-87078-490-0 (pbk. : alk. paper)
  1. Pensions—United States—Congresses. 2. Retirement income—United States—Congresses. 3. Social security—United States—Congresses. I. Ghilarducci, Teresa. II. National Academy of Social Insurance (U.S.). Conference (16th : 2004 : Washington, D.C.) III. Title.
  HD7125.I522 2004
  331.25'2'0973—dc22

                                                                    2004021294

Cover design and illustration by Claude Goodwin.

Manufactured in the United States of America.

FOREWORD

Perhaps the only two related facts that individuals on all sides of the current debate about Social Security agree upon is that the average age of the U.S. population is increasing and that there are many surviving members of the baby-boom generation. Regrettably, on many other matters, even some of those who are deemed scholars seem to find it all too easy to distort, oversimplify, and confuse both the facts and the public policy issues.

To be sure, the whole discussion has a certain artificiality since it is based on demographic and economic projections that extend far beyond a reasonable horizon—at least based on the margins of error in past analyses about the future. That caveat aside, most parties are willing to take the projections of the Social Security trustees at face value. Each year, that body projects the financial status of the program for the ensuing seventy-five years. In 2004, the Social Security actuaries estimated that the program will run a surplus until 2042 and would be able to pay out more than 70 percent of its obligations thereafter. The estimates can and do change from year to year; for example, the date of the shortfall has been pushed back every year since 1997, when it was estimated that Social Security first would be forced to reduce payments as early as 2029. It is important to note that these variations in predictions have not stemmed from major changes in the American economy or even the availability of data but rather reflect minor changes in the assumptions of economic models.

Recently, some analysts have tried to take the projections much further, claiming to forecast, in a meaningful way, the needs of Social Security for a century or more. In my view, at least, it requires a leap of faith or a rejection of common sense to assume we can have any real notion about the financial health of this program—and that of the nation—at such a distant date. Still, proponents of privatizing Social

Security have used such a model to bolster their arguments for doing away with the government-sponsored social insurance program entirely.

In general, we should be wary about those with too much confidence in their ability to predict the future. Examples abound to show just how wrong these predictions can be. In the late nineteenth century, before the advent of the automobile, airplane, television, computer, or superconductor, the commissioner of patents proposed closing his office, asserting that everything worth inventing had already been invented. More recently, during the dot-com boom, some "analysts" famously predicted that the Dow Jones Industrial Average would reach 36,000, just a short while before it lost 20 percent of its value.

Long-term economic projections tend to be based on many assumptions—economic and political—the accuracy of which economists cannot possibly guarantee. With respect to Social Security, even slight changes in estimates of the productive capacity of the economy over the next seventy-five years can lead to drastically different projections. Policy decisions by elected officials also have a tremendous potential to affect the accuracy of predictions. One need only look to the past few years for a case in point: four years ago, budget analysts were confident of a $5 trillion projected surplus by 2010. Today, we are facing a projected $5 trillion deficit over the next ten years.

Still, there are a few assumptions that can help us think more clearly about the future. We can, for example, be confident about the fact that America is aging. As baby boomers approach retirement age, the percentage of the population over age sixty-five will nearly double. We know that medical costs are rising rapidly, and if this trend goes unchecked, conflict about how to pay the bills will intensify. We know that Social Security funding and benefits are likely to need adjustments, but we also know that the program is likely to run a surplus for another four decades. Perhaps most important, we know that tens of millions of retirees continue to need a foundation of income upon which they can depend. Although Social Security was intended to be a safety net and not a primary source of income, 48 percent of current older Americans would be below the poverty line without their monthly Social Security payments. In fact, nearly 25 percent of retirees rely almost exclusively upon Social Security for their incomes.

Social Security has become even more important and necessary to millions of future recipients, as they have taken on more personal risk with respect to retirement. This is in part due to the fact that real wages have stagnated since 1973, with only top earners experiencing significant gains. Americans are saving at an all-time low, just two-thirds the rate at which we saved in the 1970s. Despite the introduction of attractive, tax-deductible savings programs, just 3 percent of Americans making less than $30,000 a year contribute to IRAs. And much employer-based pension coverage has changed in ways that add to workers' risks. Those who are covered by private programs are likely to have "defined contribution" plans, often in the form of 401(k)s, rather than the traditional "defined benefit" plans. In the latter, employers shoulder most or all of the market risk; in the former, that uncertainty is borne by workers. While 401(k)s can be an attractive option for corporations, the fate of employees at Enron and MCI WorldCom has shown just how unstable a source of retirement income they can be for employees.

This volume brings together a distinguished group of scholars whose ideas about retirement security in America run the gamut. The essays stem from the National Academy of Social Insurance's annual conference in January 2004. Though the authors do not always agree on the solutions, or even the gravity of the problems surrounding retirement security, their efforts, taken together, offer an insightful explanation of the issues confronting an aging America. The strength of this volume is not that it attempts to offer a single prescribed solution but rather that it raises questions that will foster continued debate: Should the retirement age be extended? Can we increase national savings without resorting to enforced savings? What, if any, other government programs should be cut in order to fund Social Security and Medicare? Can any form of private savings accounts work? What can we learn from the efforts of other countries to fix their own retirement plans? Do Americans still believe in a social contract between generations? Between the rich and the poor?

The authors address culturally sensitive issues of social welfare and individual responsibility thoughtfully and analytically, avoiding inflammatory language that more often is used to shape political rhetoric than to inform the debate. The editors achieve the difficult task of breaking down these complex issues and presenting them in a fashion that is useful to policymakers, advocates, and interested citizens alike. Moreover, they present uncertainties surrounding retirement security and offer a variety of means of addressing them, well aware that there is not only one right solution to the problem.

The Century Foundation and its trustees are deeply committed to supporting research and increasing public discourse on the issues covered in this book. Our earlier publications about Social Security and pension reform include *Countdown to Reform: The Great Social Security Debate* by Henry J. Aaron and Robert D. Reischauer; Robert M. Ball's *Straight Talk about Social Security;* Robert Eisner's *Social Security: More, Not Less;* Joseph White's *False Alarm: Why the Greatest Threat to Social Security and Medicare Is the Campaign to "Save" Them;* and the edited volume *Social Security Reform: Beyond the Basics.* On economic inequality, Edward Wolff's *Top Heavy* has proved informative and popular. We also sponsored a task force on Medicare in 2001 with recommendations for that program's future. In addition, we have published a series of Reality Checks, short, easy-to-read pamphlets that use graphs and tables to correct widespread misconceptions about these and other critical issues confronting our country, which are available on our Web site, www.tcf.org.

It is in the national interest to keep elderly Americans out of poverty. Franklin Delano Roosevelt referred to the Social Security Act as "a law that will take care of human needs and at the same time provide for the United States an economic structure of vastly greater soundness." The debate over the future of Social Security and Medicare is more than just political rhetoric. We must not lose sight of what is at stake.

I commend Teresa Ghilarducci, Van Doorn Ooms, John L. Palmer, and Catherine Hill for their leadership in editing this volume and the authors for their valuable contributions to our understanding of this critical social, moral, political, and economic issue.

RICHARD C. LEONE, *President*
The Century Foundation

CONTENTS

ACKNOWLEDGMENTS

This book was developed from sessions at the National Academy of Social Insurance's sixteenth annual conference, held January 22–23, 2004, at the National Press Club in Washington, D.C. The conference examined how developments in employer-sponsored pensions, disability insurance, and retiree health benefits are changing retirement prospects for millions of Americans.

As with all activities organized under its auspices, the National Academy of Social Insurance takes responsibility for ensuring the independence of this book. Participants in the conference were chosen for their recognized expertise and with due consideration of the balance of disciplines appropriate to the program. The resulting chapters are the views of the presenters and are not necessarily those of the officers, board, or members of the academy.

We appreciate the efforts of all those who made this book possible: the authors for their attention to the task of turning their presentations into chapters; Pamela Larson, Anita Cardwell, and Nelly Ganesan of the academy staff, who assisted the editors and organized the process; and Beverly Goldberg and her staff at the Century Foundation Press, especially Steven Greenfield, who edited the manuscript, Tom Helleberg, and Jason Renker.

—TG, VDO, JLP, CH

1.

INTRODUCTION

Catherine Hill, Teresa Ghilarducci, Van Doorn Ooms,
and John L. Palmer

Retirement is a relatively modern invention. Well into the twentieth century, most elderly people relied on their families when they could no longer work. Public retirement programs originated in Europe and were brought to the United States by the Roosevelt administration as part of its New Deal. Social Security, followed by the employer-based pension plans that took off after World War II and then Medicare, created new options for older Americans. Social Security and Medicare, sometimes supplemented by retiree health benefits and defined benefit pensions, became the foundations of economic security that enabled older Americans to retire with dignity and financial independence.

But social insurance and tax-advantaged retirement benefits come at a price. Today, Social Security and Medicare are facing serious financial shortfalls. Employers are struggling to keep their pensions afloat, and many companies are turning to the government (specifically the Pension Benefit Guaranty Corporation) for help in paying promised benefits to their retirees. Fewer and fewer companies are offering traditional pensions; instead, many now offer "defined contribution" plans such as 401(k) plans that are essentially individual savings accounts that have special tax advantages as well as restrictions on withdrawals. Employers also are backing away from continued health insurance coverage for their retirees, adding another financial responsibility for individuals to tackle on their own.

The push toward personal responsibility comes at a challenging time. Americans are living longer than ever before. At age sixty-five, men on average will live another sixteen years, and women age sixty-five can expect on average to live another nineteen years. Of course, about half of retirees live longer than average. At age sixty-five, about one in seven men and one in four women can expect to reach his or her ninetieth birthday, potentially spending twenty-five years or more in retirement. For individuals, longer retirements mean stretching savings over more years. For society, longer life spans mean that retirees receive benefits from public programs such as Social Security and Medicare longer, increasing the size of the population receiving benefits at any given time.

The ranks of retirees receiving Social Security and Medicare benefits will grow further as baby boomers retire. By 2020 boomers will range from ages fifty-six to seventy-four, spanning the decades during which most people retire. Between 2000 and 2020 the baby-boom bulge will double the number of Americans ages fifty-five to sixty-four from 23.6 million to about 41.5 million.

Americans depend on both government programs and individual savings when they retire. Social Security is the main source of income for most elderly people. More than 90 percent of Americans age sixty-five and older receive Social Security. For two out of three of them, Social Security is more than half of their income. For about a quarter of unmarried women, Social Security is the only source of income.

Social Security was never intended to be the sole source of income in retirement. Americans also are expected to save for their own retirement and enjoy substantial tax advantages if they do so. Yet, many workers have no access or only sporadic access to tax-favored pensions. About half of private sector workers are not covered by a pension plan at any given time. And about half of American families do not have a retirement savings account such as a 401(k) or other defined contribution pension, an individual retirement account (IRA), or a Keogh plan. Thus, many workers, including some from middle-income households, are not building up tax-favored savings to supplement Social Security in retirement.

The following six chapters provide fresh perspectives on the changing responsibilities of individuals, employees, and government. Should Social Security and Medicare reform further the shift toward personal responsibility, or should these programs continue to emphasize collective responsibility and thereby moderate changes in the private sector? Are there models of privatization that could work in the United States? Why do Americans not save more on their own? If we cannot save more, should Americans simply work longer? Can older workers compete in the job market, especially in physically arduous occupations? This volume brings answers to these questions from a variety of viewpoints.

Chapters 2 and 3 examine the case for and against postponing retirement benefits for baby boomers. Catherine Hill and Virginia P. Reno examine the financial incentives for postponing retirement. For many Americans, working longer may be a necessity as longer life expectancy, escalating health care costs, and relatively smaller Social Security checks make early retirement less affordable. However, delaying retirement is not always feasible for older Americans who suffer declining health, particularly those workers without highly valued job skills. Social Security disability insurance covers only the most severe disabilities, leaving those older workers who are neither perfectly healthy nor fully disabled without a safety net. New financial incentives to delay retirement may not be needed, according to Hill and Reno, because both "carrots" and "sticks" are already in place. Moreover, those most susceptible to the effects of the restrictive measures most immediately accessible to policymakers—such as raising the eligibility age of Medicare or Social Security—are least likely to respond to such incentives.

Joseph F. Quinn puts the case for longer careers in historical perspective. Since at least the 1940s, American men had been retiring at earlier and earlier ages. By the mid-1980s, however, the trend toward earlier and earlier retirement seems to have stopped. Since 2000 there has been a turnaround as older men remained in or returned to the workforce. Changes in employment opportunities, pensions, Social Security rules, health, and life expectancy are among the driving forces. And for many, Quinn argues, it is reasonable to expect a longer career.

Teresa Ghilarducci counters that many other older people cannot work longer and should not be expected to do so. In a wealthy country such as the United States, there is no need to put the elderly to work. In contrast to the popular perception that retirement is linked to declining health, Ghilarducci maintains that retirement can be good for older workers, citing evidence that older men slow their rate of health degeneration and older women's health status actually improves when they retire. Living longer does not necessarily translate into an ability to work longer. Just as many older people say they cannot work today as they did twenty years ago. For Ghilarducci, the call for longer careers amounts to an attack on workers' hard-won right to retire.

In Chapter 4, Robert H. Frank takes an in-depth look at why Americans do not save enough for retirement. Temptation, or the tendency to choose "smaller but immediate rewards," is part of the saving puzzle. But Americans' difficulty reining in their spending is not simply a matter of a lack of willpower. There are real consequences to not "keeping up with the Joneses." For example, it is sensible for families to spend whatever they can to secure a good education for their children. Relative social standing creates a drive to consume that is rational for the individual, even though it is irrational from a societal point of view. How can the nation call a cease-fire to this "consumption arms race?" Social Security is one way out of this trap because it forces everyone to save. The payroll tax for Social Security and Medicare essentially makes 15 percent of earnings unavailable for individual consumption by working families. These funds are thus protected from the "bidding war" for social status. Pension plans also can serve this function, although increasingly individuals can and do borrow against their 401(k) accounts. In the end, Frank argues, government intervention is needed to mediate the human tendencies to jockey for economic status and to choose short-term over long-term rewards.

In Chapter 5, Annika Sundén provides a European example of social security reform. As Sweden is often cited as a leader in innovative pension reform, it is a useful model for those considering privatizing Social Security in the United States. Sundén describes the basic features of the new Swedish pension system (the public pension system in Europe is equivalent to our own Social Security). Swedish policymakers recognized that the previous pay-as-you-go, defined benefit system was not sustainable in the long term but were unwilling to raise already high contribution rates of nearly 19 percent of payroll. In addition, benefits were only weakly linked to contributions. Beginning a sixteen-year phase-in in 1999, the new, two-tier system combines a pay-as-you-go Notional Defined Contribution (NDC) plan with funded individual accounts. While the new system directly links benefits to contributions, a generous minimum pension funded from general revenues provides significant redistribution. The NDC has several automatic mechanisms that adjust benefits to ensure the long-term stability of the system, thereby preventing the contribution rate from rising and insulating the system from political intervention. Sundén is careful to note, however, that the new system will not in itself eliminate the pressures associated with the baby boomers' retirement, which will be financed in part by the "buffer funds" accumulated under the previous system.

Is saving for retirement solely an individual responsibility, or is there a role for government? Chapter 6 pulls together four perspectives on individual and collective obligations. Maya C. MacGuineas looks at the big picture: what percentage of the economy's resources ought to be devoted to retirement provision; who should pay how much; how should the risks associated with retirement finance be distributed; and should government or businesses bear primary responsibility for direct provision of retirement benefits or can tax incentives largely accomplish the same goals. MacGuineas favors a shift from a system of universal benefits to one of true social insurance, emphasizing need rather than age as the fundamental criterion. She favors greater flexibility of retirement ages and the introduction of individual private accounts to supplement or replace current government retirement programs.

William A. Niskanen of the Cato Institute argues that retirement planning is principally an individual responsibility. He points to the financial problems facing social insurance programs as evidence against government involvement. Overall he favors a defined contribution approach that maximizes individual choice. John H. Langbein agrees that social insurance programs (like Social Security and Medicare) interfere with individual freedom but claims that this infringement is a necessary one. People simply do not save adequately for retirement on their own. Social Security also plays an important redistributive function at a juncture in life when there are few other options for maintaining living standards. Social Security has greatly reduced poverty among the elderly and should be viewed as one of the great success stories of American government. Langbein concludes that "there are limits for free markets, and this is one of them."

Jerry L. Mashaw believes that there may be middle ground to be found in pondering the values behind social insurance. For the most part, Americans believe that everyone (at least every healthy adult) is responsible for his or her own economic well-being. However, in a modern society, no man or woman is an island. A substantial share of the nation's wealth stems from collective endeavors, but individuals reap very different rewards for their work in a market economy. Social insurance helps to preserve social harmony in the face of inequality. By shoring up income at times of unemployment and in retirement, as well as providing basic health care for the elderly, social insurance helps make inequality more palatable. Equally important, it helps to spread the risk of high-cost setbacks such as chronic illnesses or career-ending disabilities across society. Many Americans agree with these basic goals associated with social insurance, contends Mashaw, though they are deeply divided on how to achieve them.

In Chapter 7, Lawrence H. Thompson reconsiders the question of intergenerational equity by examining how future economic growth could affect the relative living standards of future workers and retirees. Using the official projections of the Medicare and Social Security trustees through 2030, he finds that, under current policies, workers will enjoy the gains of economic growth, while retirees will lag behind. Benefit cuts already enacted and rising out-of-pocket health care spending indicate that the average retiree at age sixty-five in 2030 will have net income that is 3 percent lower than in 2003. At the same time, rising real wages mean that the average worker by 2030 will have wages that are 32 percent higher than in 2003. Thompson concludes that the fruits of economic growth would be more equally shared between workers and retirees if the current financing gaps in Social Security and Medicare were bridged by tax increases rather than by additional benefit cuts. He estimates that a tax increase sufficient to balance both Social Security and Medicare and support a partial prescription drug benefit would result in workers enjoying a 21 percent hike in their net wages, while retirees would enjoy an 18 percent increase in their net benefits. In further pursuing the question about fairness between generations, Thompson compares the size of economic transfers within households when children are young and the transfers from adult children to aging parents through financing Social Security and Medicare. He concludes that the children would still be net recipients of transfers between generations, even if they paid the additional payroll taxes needed to support the retirement of their parents' generation.

CONCLUSIONS

Social Security and Medicare have enabled far more Americans than ever to retire with dignity and financial independence. The evolving public system effectively socializes and institutionalizes the support of retired workers (and their surviving partners) that, in earlier times, was provided in the form of shared living quarters and direct aid to aging parents. Today workers support everyone's aged relatives and, in turn, expect everyone's children to support them when they retire. A universal system pools risk broadly and thereby protects everyone against financial hardship in old age, with substantial economic and social benefits. This form of cross-generational social insurance is an essential underpinning of a highly mobile and innovative workforce.

Most Americans understand the "social contract" to involve relationships within as well as across generations. What obligations do we owe to others in our society outside the circle of family and friends? Individualism and the rewards to personal endeavor appear to run stronger in our diverse society and market-oriented economy than in most other industrialized nations. But economic rewards are not created by individual endeavor alone. Success also depends upon laws and institutions that protect property, business relationships that promote cooperation and trust, the fit between one's personal capacities and the public's demand for goods and services, and often simply luck, especially with regard to the circumstances of birth and early development. For this reason, the soundness of a capitalist economy that produces substantial inequality requires a safety net that encompasses social insurance for "ordinary" risks such as retirement as well as welfare for those in dire need.

The balance between personal and collective responsibility for retirement planning is likely to remain a topic of public debate. Just as the world of work is constantly changing, so too will options for retirement.

Myriad publications have been written promoting policy options for restoring solvency to Social Security and Medicare and dealing with the financial woes of pension providers as well as offering advice on strategies to encourage individuals to save more for retirement. This volume takes a step back to look at the big picture, offering new ways of thinking about the changing responsibilities of individuals, employers, and governments for financing retirement.

2.

THE FINANCIAL CASE FOR LATE RETIREMENT

Catherine Hill and Virginia P. Reno

Retirement is not what it used to be, and this may come as a surprise to some baby boomers approaching retirement. This chapter presents a case for delaying retirement from both an individual and a societal perspective and argues that incentives for delaying retirement are already in place. It explores why the public does not fully appreciate them. Two of the stumbling blocks for individuals contemplating their financial future may be the tendency to overlook how inflation will erode purchasing power over time and the tendency to overrate the value of a lump-sum account in providing long-term retirement security. Thus, many people fail to respond to the financial incentives to delay retirement, not because such incentives are lacking but because they are insufficiently appreciated. Finally, while working longer makes good economic sense, it is not for everyone. A strong safety net is needed that fully accounts for differences in the job prospects for older workers in different circumstances.

The call for later retirement has been put forward by many observers. The financial challenges facing Social Security and Medicare in the coming decades are well established, although experts disagree on the severity of the situation. By 2030 more than 20 percent of Americans will be age sixty-five and older, rising from 12 percent of the population in 2000. The first baby boomers will become eligible for Social Security in 2008 and Medicare in 2011, and all boomers will be eligible for these programs by 2030.

According to the Social Security trustees, tax revenue paid into the trust funds is projected to be less than the benefit payments due in 2018. Interest on the reserves and the assets themselves will continue to supplement tax revenue until 2042, when the Social Security reserves are likely to be depleted. Income supporting the Social Security program is expected to cover about 72 percent of benefit obligations at that time. As the trustees note in their 2004 annual report, "In just 20 years, OASDI [Social Security] will go from providing annual surplus revenue to the Treasury equal to 7 percent of Federal income taxes to requiring a transfer from the Treasury—to redeem bonds that comprise the trust fund reserves—equal to more than 6 percent of Federal income taxes (projected at their historical share of GDP)."

Medicare's financial problems are larger, and shortfalls are expected to occur sooner. While both programs confront essentially the same demographic issues, Medicare faces the additional challenge that health care costs are projected to rise more rapidly than wages (and the payroll taxes based on these wages). The new Medicare prescription drug benefit will add to the overall cost of Medicare and will increase the proportion of total Medicare costs financed from federal general fund revenues.

Delaying the age of eligibility for Medicare or further delaying the age of eligibility for full Social Security benefits could reduce outlays, assuming new benefits were not adjusted upward in response. One study found that raising the age of Medicare eligibility to sixty-seven could lower outlays by about $28 billion a year (in 2000 dollars), by essentially shifting costs to employer-based health plans, Medicaid, and individuals.[1] For Social Security, the rise in the age of eligibility for full benefits from sixty-five to sixty-seven is expected to result in approximately a 13 percent cut (on average) for benefits claimed at any age.

The financial problems facing Medicare and Social Security lead some observers to advocate working longer and delaying retirement as a way to reduce the number of beneficiaries and increase the number of workers paying taxes. But is it reasonable to expect everyone to work well into their sixties? Are there jobs for all these older workers? And, finally, why do people fail to appreciate the financial incentives to work longer that are already in place? These questions will be revisited after an exploration of the financial case for late retirement.

TABLE 2.1. LIFE EXPECTANCY* AT AGE 65, 1940–2020

Year	Men	Women
1940	11.9	13.4
1960	12.9	15.9
1980	14.0	18.4
2000	15.8	18.9
2020	17.0	19.9

*Period life expectancy. The average years of life remaining if sixty-five-year-olds in that year were to experience the mortality rates for that year over the remainder of their lives.

Source: Trustees of the Federal Old-Age and Survivors and Disability Insurance Trust Funds, Social Security Administration, 2003 Annual Report.

LIFE EXPECTANCY IS INCREASING

Americans are living longer, and gains in life expectancy are projected to continue. The question is whether the extended life spans will be spent in retirement or in longer careers or will be shared between both. Between 1940 and 1980 life expectancy at age sixty-five increased by 2.1 years for men and 5.0 years for women, and further increases were predicted. Increasing life spans led policymakers in 1983 to shore up Social Security's future finances by gradually raising the age at which full benefits would be paid. Those changes are starting to take effect now and will continue over the next twenty years. During the next two decades, it is anticipated that life expectancy will continue to increase, by about 1.0 year for women and 1.2 years for men (see Table 2.1).

OLDER AMERICANS ARE BECOMING MORE INDEPENDENT

Some evidence indicates that Americans age sixty-five and older are becoming healthier, measured in terms of the ability to live independently. David Cutler finds that the prevalence of dependency among the elderly declined during the 1980s and 1990s.[2] Dependency is defined in terms of difficulty with basic activities of daily living—such as eating, bathing, dressing, and getting around— and what are termed instrumental activities of daily living—doing light housework, shopping, preparing meals, and so on. National surveys show that dependency declined among the young elderly (ages sixty-five to seventy-four) as well as among those at older ages. Cutler attributes the improvements to a variety of causes, including innovations in medical care like joint replacements and cataract surgery that restore functioning and new drug therapies that prevent some of the disabling consequences of arthritis and heart disease.

Wider use of technology and the choice of more convenience items also may contribute to greater independence among the elderly. Architectural changes following the Americans with Disabilities Act of 1990—such as handrails, ramps, walk-in showers, and single-story housing or condominiums with elevators—enable more elderly people to perform activities of daily living in their own homes without assistance. Developments in the kitchen like microwave ovens and prepackaged meals simplify meal preparations. Environmental changes—curb cuts, accessible transportation, and so forth—make it possible for more elderly to shop and otherwise get out and about on their own.

THE LABOR FORCE WILL GROW MORE SLOWLY OVER THE NEXT TWENTY YEARS

Over the next twenty years the American labor force will change in ways very different from the past. Between 1980 and 2000 the number of workers expanded rapidly. The total workforce grew by 35 percent, and the so-called prime-age workforce (between ages twenty-five and fifty-four) burgeoned by a remarkable 54 percent. The two decades to come portend a very different tale. The workforce will grow more slowly. The prime-age workforce will increase hardly at all. Almost all the growth will be among those age fifty-five and older and foreign-born labor.[3]

THE NUMBER OF COLLEGE-EDUCATED WORKERS WILL GROW MORE SLOWLY

Gains in educational attainment of the workforce will be smaller in the future than in the recent past. Over the past twenty years the size of the college-educated workforce has grown rapidly. Between 1980 and 2000 the number of workers with college degrees more than doubled; as a share of the workforce, they grew from 22 to 30 percent. Over the next twenty years gains in educational attainment are projected to be modest. At best, college graduates might increase from 30 to 35 percent of the workforce.[4] With no increase in higher education graduation rates, graduates will remain about 31 percent of the workforce.

What do these two forecasts imply about opportunities to work longer? First, they suggest that if the country does have a tight labor market in the future, employers will be more likely than in the past to seek out older workers. Second, it suggests that college-educated workers may have more job opportunities because a crowd of similarly educated workers will not be queuing up to replace them.

EMPLOYERS MAY WANT TO KEEP SKILLED OLDER WORKERS

American employers have a successful track record of adapting to a changing workforce. Accommodating the large influx of younger baby boomers and women of all ages into the workforce in the 1970s and 1980s is a case in point. One of the ways businesses made room for new workers was by encouraging early retirement. The rapid growth of young entrants made it popular with all concerned to have corporate policies that encouraged early retirement. Older workers found early retirement affordable and attractive when pensions and retiree health benefits were available. Younger workers found opportunities for advancement as older workers retired, and employers were able to replace older workers with younger, less expensive ones. In the coming two decades slower growth in the workforce, and in the ranks of the college-educated in particular, could strengthen the business case for encouraging skilled and experienced mature employees to stay with their firms.[5]

FINANCIAL INCENTIVES TO WORK LONGER

Working longer means higher incomes, greater access to health insurance, and better security upon retirement. The advantage of a later retirement has been strengthened in recent years by changes in Social Security and pensions. Uncertainty about ability to afford long-term care and to meet obligations for out-of-pocket health costs add to the financial case for working longer if one is able to do so.

Medicare, together with Social Security, provides the foundation of financial security for older Americans. Yet, elderly Americans still pay a considerable amount out of their own pockets for health care. Out-of-pocket spending goes for Medicare premiums, deductibles, and coinsurance, services that Medicare does not cover, and premiums for supplemental health coverage from employer plans or Medigap insurance. Average out-of-pocket spending was about $3,140 in 2000 (see Table 2.2). Over the next twenty-five years real out-of-pocket spending is projected to rise by 67 percent, increasing from 22 to 30 percent of the incomes of the elderly.[6]

HEALTH CARE BILLS ARE THE BIG UNKNOWN FOR FUTURE RETIREES

Paying for health care is the wild card in trying to anticipate future retirement needs, according to a recent study by the Employee Benefit Research Institute.[7] The individual health care burden is large and highly unpredictable. Even with Medicare and employer-based retiree coverage, an individual retiring at age sixty-five in 2003 could need a nest egg of between $37,000 and $750,000 (net present value) to pay for expenses not covered by Medicare or the employer plan. According to Paul Fronstin and Dallas Salisbury's estimates, the same individual without employer-sponsored coverage

TABLE 2.2. OUT-OF-POCKET SPENDING FOR MEDICARE BENEFICIARIES, 2000 AND 2025

Category of Beneficiaries	2000	2025
Annual amount (in 2000 dollars)		
All elderly beneficiaries	$3,142	$5,248
Elderly with poor health and no additional insurance	$4,478	$7,263
Low-income unmarried women over age 85 in poor health	$5,969	$9,378
As a percentage of income		
All elderly beneficiaries	22	30
Elderly with poor health and no additional insurance	44	63
Low-income unmarried women over age 85 in poor health	52	72

Source: Stephanie Maxwell, Marilyn Moon, and Misha Segal, "Growth in Medicare and Out-of-Pocket Spending: Impact on Vulnerable Beneficiaries," Urban Institute, Washington, D.C., 2001.

to supplement Medicare could need between $47,000 and $1,458,000 to cover out-of-pocket costs. Expenses for long-term care are not included in these estimates and could add considerably to costs for retirees. Services such as nursing home care typically cost about $50,000 a year.[8]

PAYING FOR LONG-TERM CARE IS A GROWING REALITY

The prospect of needing, and paying for, their own long-term care is a growing reality for baby boomers. Some are learning firsthand that Medicare does not pay for such care. Many baby boomers are now coping with tending to their aging parents, often with the help of siblings.

Realizing they have more siblings than offspring can be a sobering prospect as boomers contemplate their own future vulnerability. Smaller families and a higher incidence of divorce may mean that more boomers will need to pay nonrelatives for care in advanced old age. Working longer may be the only way to build financial protection against those costs.

SOCIAL SECURITY INCENTIVES TO DELAY RETIREMENT ARE PHASING IN

Changes taking place in Social Security now are enhancing the financial advantage of delaying retirement and stiffening the penalty for retiring early. These changes were enacted in 1983 and are being phased in over the next two decades.

Delaying retirement brings higher monthly benefits. Retirees have a choice to claim Social Security between ages sixty-two (the earliest eligibility age) and seventy (after which there is no advantage to further delay). Monthly benefits are higher if one waits to claim Social Security at the so-called normal retirement age (which has long been sixty-five) and are further increased if one waits until seventy to claim benefits. A worker who took Social Security benefits at age sixty-two in 1999 would get monthly benefits permanently reduced to 80 percent of what would have been paid if he or she waited until age sixty-five. By waiting until age seventy, the benefit would be 132.5 percent of what would have been paid at sixty-five (see Figure 2.1). Postponing retirement until seventy causes the monthly benefit to be about 66 percent larger than it would have been had the retiree taken benefits at age sixty-two. In Figure 2.1, the dark bars illustrate how benefits increase as workers delay claiming them between ages sixty-two and seventy.

   The premium associated with delaying retirement is calculated after figuring in the annual cost-of-living increase for those taking early retirement. For example, a retiree who took a $1,000 monthly benefit at age sixty-two and had a 3 percent cost of living increase each year would receive $1,267 a month at age seventy. If, instead, the worker had waited until age seventy to draw Social Security, the benefit would be $2,098 a month. The gain in monthly income would be $831 a month—an increase of 66 percent over taking benefits at age sixty-two.

FIGURE 2.1. SOCIAL SECURITY BENEFITS WITH NORMAL RETIREMENT AGE (NRA) AT 65 AND 67

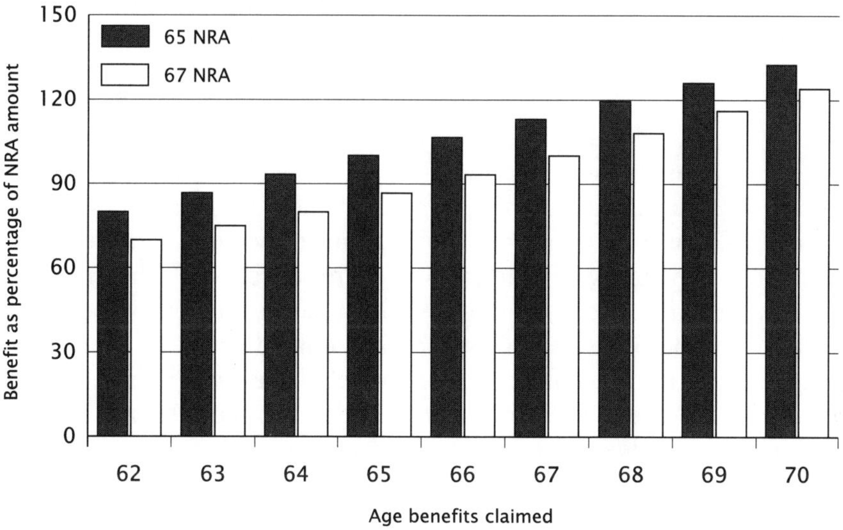

Source: Authors' calculations.

Early retirement benefits will be reduced in the future. Policies enacted in 1983 called for gradually raising the normal Social Security retirement age from sixty-five to sixty-seven. Social Security is still available at age sixty-two, but the reduction in benefits claimed will be larger. The normal retirement age is rising to sixty-six for people who reach their sixty-second birthday between 2005 and 2016 and will rise again to sixty-seven for people who reach their sixty-second birthday between 2017 and 2022. By then, benefits claimed at sixty-two will be reduced to 70 percent of the full benefit amount, and benefits claimed at age sixty-five will be cut to 87 percent. Benefits claimed after the normal retirement age will still be increased, by a full 8 percent for each year that benefits are delayed up to age seventy. When the normal retirement age reaches sixty-seven, a retiree who waits until age seventy to claim benefits will receive about 177 percent of what would be received if departure from the workforce had occurred at sixty-two. As shown by the light bars in Figure 2.1, raising the normal retirement age is equivalent to an across-the-board cut in monthly Social Security benefits at any age.

Social Security will replace a smaller share of retirees' prior earnings.
In the future, Social Security benefits will be lower relative to workers' earnings than they are today for three reasons. First, the increase in the normal retirement age will lower the retiree's replacement rate, that is, the portion of past earnings that Social Security benefits replace. Second, premiums that beneficiaries pay for Part B of Medicare are deducted from Social Security benefits. Because Medicare premiums will grow faster than benefits, they will take a bigger bite out of future Social Security benefits. Third, rules enacted in 1983 for making part of Social Security benefits subject to the federal income tax will gradually affect more retirees. The taxation of benefits affects only people whose incomes are above certain thresholds. Because the thresholds are not adjusted to keep pace with growth in the economy, more beneficiaries will be affected as their incomes rise in line with overall wages or prices. Alicia Munnell estimates how these changes will affect benefits and replacement rates for a middle-ranking earner by 2030 (see Table 2.3). Today a median earner (making about $34,000 a year) who retired at age sixty-five would receive Social Security benefits that replace about 39 percent of past earnings after deducting the Medicare premium. A similar worker who retired at age sixty-five in 2030 would get net Social Security benefits that replace only about 30 percent of prior earnings, a drop in the replacement rate of slightly more than 20 percent.

CHANGES IN PENSION PLANS PUT
MORE RESPONSIBILITY ON WORKERS

One of the most dramatic changes in the economy over the past two decades has been the substitution of defined contribution pensions such as 401(k)s for traditional defined benefit pension plans.[9] Defined benefit plans were common in the 1970s and 1980s. Today employee-directed defined contribution plans are the dominant form. This shift eliminates incentives for early retirement found in some defined benefit pension plans. In addition to eliminating incentives for early retirement, this change profoundly alters the responsibilities of individuals for their own retirements.

**TABLE 2.3. CHANGES IN SOCIAL SECURITY BENEFITS RELATIVE TO
EARNINGS FOR A TYPICAL WORKER,* 2000 AND 2030**

Year and Reason for Change	Benefits Relative to Earnings (replacement rate in percent)
Retiree in 2000	41.2
Net, after deducting Part B premium	38.7
Retiree in 2030	
After raising normal retirement age	36.5
Net, after deducting Part B premium	33.2
Net, after personal income tax**	30.5
Percentage change in net replacement rate	(21)

*A typical worker earned slightly less than $34,000 in 2002.

**Social Security benefits after the income taxation of benefits (and after subtracting Part B premium) divided by previous earnings before tax.

Source: Alicia H. Munnell, "The Declining Role of Social Security," *Just the Facts on Retirement Issues* (Center for Retirement Research at Boston College), no. 6, February 2003, available online at http://www.bc.edu/centers/crr/facts/jtf_6.pdf.

SHIFT TOWARD GREATER PERSONAL RESPONSIBILITY FOR RETIREMENT

Defined benefit pensions are usually financed solely by employers and are designed to supplement Social Security. They are called "defined benefit" because the employer is responsible for paying a specified benefit, usually based on the worker's length of service and covered wages. Benefits are typically paid as monthly amounts and last for the life of the retiree (and usually for a widowed spouse, unless the spouse were to decline survivor benefits).

Defined contribution plans, including the increasingly popular 401(k) plans, do not promise a specified benefit. Instead, employees bear the risk that funds contributed to their accounts, plus investment earnings (or losses), will fall short of producing an adequate supplement to Social Security. Defined contribution plans usually pay lump sums when an employee leaves the plan. Workers can roll over

FIGURE 2.2. PENSION COVERAGE TRENDS, 1979–1998
PRIVATE WAGE AND SALARY WORKERS

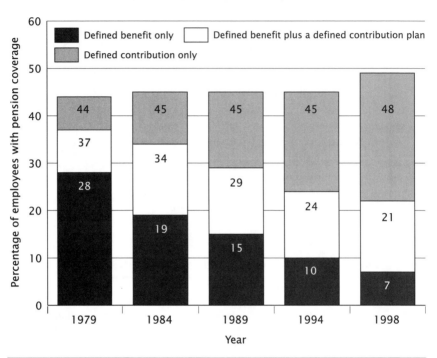

Source: U.S. Department of Labor, Pension and Welfare Benefits Administration, Private Pension Plan Bulletin, *Abstract of 1998 Form 5550, Annual Reports,* Number 11, Winter 2001–2002, pp. 81 and 82.

the money into an individual retirement account (IRA) or other tax-deferred retirement plan to avoid paying taxes on the funds until they retire.

Traditional defined benefit pension plans are covering ever fewer private sector workers, while defined contribution coverage is growing. Between 1979 and 1998 the share of private sector workers covered by defined benefit plans fell from 37 to 21 percent. The proportion of workers with only defined contribution coverage jumped from 7 to 27 percent. Workers with supplemental defined contribution coverage, usually a 401(k) plan on top of a defined benefit plan, also became more common—rising from 9 percent of private employees in 1979 to 14–15 percent in every year since (see Figure 2.2).

**TABLE 2.4. AVERAGE LIFE EXPECTANCY AND
PROBABILITY OF LIVING TO AGE 90**

Age in 1999	Average Life Expectancy (in years)		Probability of Living to Age 90 (in percent)	
	Men	*Women*	*Men*	*Women*
55	78.2	82.1	12.4	25.0
65	80.7	83.9	14.2	27.0
70	82.5	85.3	16.2	29.3

Source: Authors' calculations based on period life tables, *Statistical Supplement to the Social Security Bulletin,* 2002, generated from data from the National Center for Health Statistics and the U.S. Census Bureau.

WHY PEOPLE DO NOT FULLY APPRECIATE INCENTIVES TO DELAY RETIREMENT

A number of human traits make it difficult for individual retirees to ensure that their defined contribution accounts provide financial security for the rest of their lives. First, as workers in their fifties and early sixties think about retirement, it is difficult to anticipate what life will be like twenty or thirty years down the road. For fifty-five-year-olds, an average man can expect to live another twenty-three years and an average woman another twenty-seven years (see Table 2.4). But no one can know for sure. About one in eight men and one in four women at the age of fifty-five can expect to reach their ninetieth birthday. Thirty-five years is a very long planning horizon. At age fifty-five, the prospect of ninety is as far off as one's twentieth birthday is in the past.

UNDERSTANDING WEALTH ILLUSION AND MONEY ILLUSION

With traditional defined benefit pensions, retirees can readily find out the size of the monthly pension available at different retirement ages and decide when they can afford to retire. Lump-sum payments from defined contribution plans can greatly complicate the question of when one can afford to retire. Two common tendencies make this difficult. First, it is easy to be misled by "wealth illusion"—that is, to place a much higher value on a pot of money in hand than on an equivalent amount that is guaranteed to be paid in regular installments for the rest of one's life. Second, "money illusion" refers to the difficulty of anticipating the adverse effect on purchasing power of even modest rates of inflation over a long period of time.

Wealth illusion makes a lump sum look big relative to what it will buy over a lifetime. To illustrate the wealth illusion trade-off, consider a fifty-five-year-old who had the option to retire and cash out a lump-sum balance of $100,000. That may seem like a lot of money—particularly for one accustomed to earning, say, $35,000 a year. But it looks much smaller when converted into a monthly income that would be guaranteed for the rest of that person's life. The $100,000 would be equivalent to a guaranteed income of $570 a month, or about $6,850 a year (see Table 2.5).

Money illusion overlooks how inflation will erode purchasing power over time. Even a modest rate of inflation eats away at a guaranteed income over a long period. With annual inflation of just 3 percent, purchasing power would fall by about 26 percent in ten years. After twenty-five years, purchasing power would drop 55 percent. For a fifty-five-year-old contemplating retirement now, the purchasing power of a fixed income purchased with $100,000 would start out at $6,850 a year and decline to about $3,000 a year by the time he or she turned eighty. If the retiree should live until ninety, the value of the fixed monthly income would shrink to about $2,400 a year.

Delaying retirement can improve the lasting power of pension assets. If the fifty-five-year-old had a choice to work longer and build up more in the retirement plan before cashing it out, long-term financial security would be improved. If employee and employer each continued to put 5 percent of salary into the retirement plan and the funds earned a 5 percent annual return, the account would grow to about $210,000 by the time the worker reached sixty-five.[10] Then it would be equivalent to a guaranteed annual income of about $18,050 a year.[11] Inflation would still sap the value of a fixed

TABLE 2.5. ILLUSTRATING THE FINANCIAL CASE FOR LATER RETIREMENT THREE SCENARIOS: TO RETIRE AT AGE 55, AGE 65, OR AGE 70*

Financial Outcomes of Retirement Decisions	Retire at 55	Retire at 65	Retire at 70
Unveiling Wealth Illusion			
Size of retirement plan assets	$100,000	$210,000	$289,000
Equivalent guaranteed annual income for life (at retirement)**	$6,852	$18,048	$27,924
Unveiling Money Illusion			
Purchasing power of guaranteed income (with 3 percent inflation) by:			
Age 65	$5,098	$18,048	N/A
Age 70	$4,398	$15,568	$27,924
Age 80	$3,005	$11,584	$20,781
Age 90	$2,435	$8,620	$15,461

*Key assumptions: Fifty-five-year-old, earning $35,000 with $100,000 in retirement plan. Employer and worker each contribute 5 percent of pay to the retirement plan up to retirement. Assets earn 5 percent return.

**Fixed life annuities available from the federal employees' Thrift Savings Plan, based on the annuity calculator at www.tsp.gov. Annuities based on a 4 percent interest assumption, effective in March–April 2003.

Source: Authors' calculations.

income. By age eighty purchasing power would decline by one-third to about $11,585 a year. That would be nearly four times as much, though, as the retiree would have had at that age having left work at age fifty-five.

Waiting until age seventy to quit would further improve long-range financial security. By then, assuming continued contributions and a 5 percent annual investment return, the account would grow to about $289,000, which would be equivalent to a fixed income of nearly $28,000 a year. By age eighty the purchasing power would be about $20,780.

In brief, working longer and retiring later improves financial prospects in retirement in several ways. More contributions and an extended period of investment returns increase the funds available for retirement. At the same time, a longer career shortens the period over which retirement income must be spread and lessens the period of exposure to inflation. These principles are true whether an individual purchases an annuity or draws down his or her investment through periodic calls on a lump-sum payment.

SUMMARY

Financial incentives for baby boomers to work longer and retire later are in place. Delaying retirement between ages sixty-two and seventy will increase Social Security benefits more substantially than in the past. On the flip side, Social Security benefits for future retirees will replace a smaller share of preretirement earnings if workers do not delay retirement. Defined contribution pensions or personal savings last longer if not drawn upon until later. Rising out-of-pocket health care costs and the prospect of paying for long-term care make it prudent for individuals to delay retirement if they have the opportunity to do so. Increasingly, the cards are stacked in favor of working longer.

But not all baby boomers can be expected to work through their mid-sixties. Some will experience career-ending disabilities. Others will have health problems that do not meet the strict test of disability for Social Security benefits yet have disadvantages in the labor market. As Teresa Ghilarducci reports in the next chapter, just as many older people say they are unable to work now as older workers said twenty years ago. The risk of career-ending disability faces all Americans. But the risk is greater for people with limited educations who do hard jobs. An accountant, stockbroker, or college professor faces the risk that cancer or heart disease will cut short his or her work life. A meatpacker, waitress, bricklayer, or hospital orderly also faces those risks. They face the added risk that other conditions—such as arthritis, back injuries, weakened wrists or knees—will make them unable to do the work that they do without imposing undue burdens on their coworkers, employers, customers, or patients. A safety net remains essential for those who cannot work and those who should not be expected to do so.

3.

CAN AMERICANS WORK LONGER?
COMPETING VIEWS

Joseph F. Quinn and Teresa Ghilarducci

AMERICANS CAN WORK LONGER

Joseph F. Quinn

Can Americans work longer? Are older Americans already working longer than they used to? Do they want to work longer? Is it good that older Americans are working longer? In many cases, the answer to these questions is yes. Hill and Reno in Chapter 2 make the case that, for most Americans, delaying the age of retirement makes good personal financial sense if workers have a choice. Thus, it is good news that public policy and the labor markets have encouraged Americans to work longer since the 1980s.

This issue can be put in perspective by reviewing retirement trends in the United States over the past half-century. These are readily divided into two sub-periods: 1950 to the mid-1980s and from then to the present.

The first thirty-five years of the past half-century, from 1950 through the mid-1980s, were part of a very long-term trend toward earlier and earlier retirement by older American men. Dora Costa

TABLE 3.1. MALE LABOR FORCE PARTICIPATION RATES BY AGE, 1950–2003

Year	55	60	62	65	68	70	72
1950	90.6	84.7	81.2	71.7	57.7	49.8	39.3
1960	92.8	85.9	79.8	56.8	42.0	37.2	28.0
1970	91.8	83.9	73.8	49.9	37.7	30.1	24.8
1975	87.6	76.9	64.4	39.4	23.7	23.7	22.6
1980	84.9	74.0	56.8	35.2	24.1	21.3	17.0
1985	83.7	71.0	50.9	30.5	20.5	15.9	14.9
1990	85.3	70.5	52.5	31.9	23.4	17.1	16.4
1995	81.1	68.9	51.3	33.5	22.4	20.6	16.0
2000	79.8	66.2	53.0	35.9	28.1	20.2	18.5
2001	82.0	69.5	54.4	37.5	24.5	22.9	15.8
2002	82.3	68.2	57.1	38.9	30.1	18.4	19.0
2003	81.7	69.0	56.3	39.7	29.2	22.6	17.5

Source: Bureau of Labor Statistics Web site, available online at http://stats.bls .gov.

has documented this tendency as far back as 1880.[1] This extended period witnessed steady and significant declines in the labor force participation rates of older American men.

Table 3.1 shows male participation rates for specific ages, from 1950 through 1985 and then up to the present. Among men, labor force participation at age seventy dropped from 50 to 16 percent between 1950 and 1985. Among sixty-five-year-old men, those old enough to receive full Social Security benefits, participation declined by well more than half, from 72 to 30 percent, during that same period. After 1961, when men first became eligible for early Social Security benefits at age sixty-two, the male labor force participation rate for sixty-two-year-olds declined, from 80 to 50 percent by the mid-1980s.

Similar patterns are found in data for five-year age cohorts of older men, from 1964 (when these data begin) through the mid-1980s. Among men who were sixty to sixty-four, or early retirement age, a steady decline, almost a straight-line falloff averaging about one percentage point per year, took place (see Figure 3.1). Among slightly older men, ages sixty-five to sixty-nine, a similar decline occurred, though not quite as steady, still averaging almost a percentage point per year over two decades (see Figure 3.2).

**FIGURE 3.1. LABOR FORCE PARTICIPATION RATES, MALES,
AGED 60–64, 1964–1985 (ACTUAL AND FITTED VALUES)**

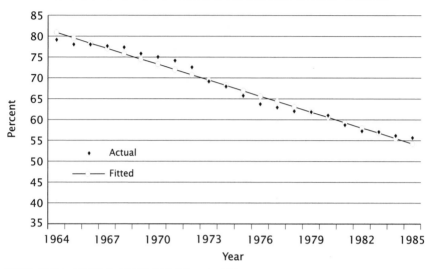

Source: Author's calculations from the Bureau of Labor Statistics Web site, available online at http://stats.bls.gov.

**FIGURE 3.2. LABOR FORCE PARTICIPATION RATES, MALES,
AGED 65–69, 1964–1985 (ACTUAL AND FITTED VALUES)**

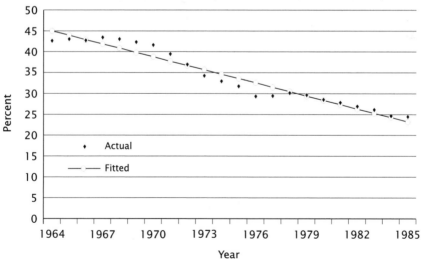

Source: Author's calculations from the Bureau of Labor Statistics Web site, available online at http://stats.bls.gov.

If one defines the median age of retirement as the age at which half the individuals are in the labor force and half are out, this was age seventy in 1950. By 1970 that 50 percent labor force participation rate appeared at age sixty-five, and by 1985 at age sixty-two. Thus, the median age of retirement dropped by eight years in only three and a half decades.

This important and far-reaching demographic phenomenon spawned considerable research to explain why men were retiring earlier and earlier, much of it focused on the increasing wealth of the population, some of which was "spent" on additional leisure late in life. Other studies examined important financial retirement incentives (or, equivalently, work disincentives) that are buried in public and private pension plans.[2]

How were American women faring during this period? In contrast to what was developing among older men, there was very little change in their labor force participation. Two important demographic trends were offsetting each other: the earlier retirement of older Americans and a significant influx of women (mostly married women) entering the labor market. For older women, these trends nearly cancelled out, as seen in Figures 3.3 and 3.4, which show data for females aged fifty-five to fifty-nine and those sixty to sixty-four years old. The net change is on the order of one percentage point per decade, not per year as observed among the men.

What has happened since the mid-1980s to the retirement climate? There has been a stunning turnaround. The relative attractiveness of work vis-à-vis leisure late in life has been altered in important ways by both governmental and private sector practices that favor longer careers, and people have responded as one would expect.

During much of the past two decades the U.S. economy performed well. The unemployment rate declined from 10 percent in 1982 to about 5 percent in 1989 and then approached 4 percent by the end of the 1990s. There was high demand for labor of all types. That was good news for those older Americans who wanted to keep working.

Unfortunately, the economy and labor demand are cyclical, and this kind of good news comes and goes. But in addition to these macroeconomic tides, there have been many important structural changes that are more permanent in nature. For example, the earliest legal age for mandatory retirement policies was raised from sixty-five to seventy in 1978, and then mandatory retirement was outlawed for a vast majority of American workers in 1986. That also was a boon for those who wanted to keep working.

FIGURE 3.3. LABOR FORCE PARTICIPATION RATES, FEMALES, AGED 55–59, 1964–1985 (ACTUAL AND FITTED VALUES)

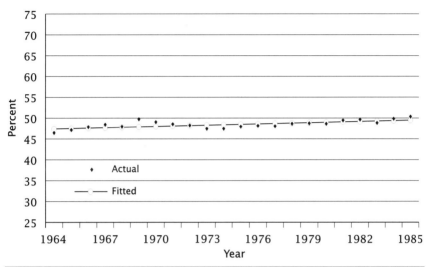

Source: Author's calculations from the Bureau of Labor Statistics Web site, available online at http://stats.bls.gov.

FIGURE 3.4. LABOR FORCE PARTICIPATION RATES, FEMALES, AGED 60–64, 1964–1985 (ACTUAL AND FITTED VALUES)

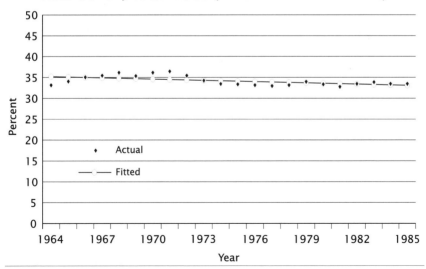

Source: Author's calculations from the Bureau of Labor Statistics Web site, available online at http://stats.bls.gov.

There also were significant changes in Social Security legislation. Strong work disincentives, inherent in the benefit calculation regulations, that kicked in at age sixty-five have been eliminated. Under prior rules, those who kept working and chose to delay their Social Security benefits had lower expected lifetime benefits than if they had stopped work and claimed benefits at age sixty-five. Their future annual benefits increased because of the additional years of work but not enough to make up for the benefits forgone. Over time, the "delayed retirement credit" has been increased, and it is now close to actuarially fair for the average worker, which means that the projected benefits for someone with an average life expectancy no longer decline with additional work after age sixty-five. This is more good news for those who want to keep working.

In addition, the normal retirement age is being increased to age sixty-six and later will rise further, to sixty-seven. This is equivalent to an across-the-board decrease in Social Security benefits. It is difficult to call this good news for older workers, but, like the other changes mentioned above, it makes retirement less attractive and work more attractive at the margin.

On the employer front, there has been a dramatic movement toward defined contribution benefit plans and away from defined benefit plans. Why is this important?

Traditional defined benefit employer pension plans typically have very strong, age-specific financial penalties for workers who stay on the job too long, just like Social Security used to. A worker's expected lifetime pension benefit usually declines with continued work after some age, often the earliest age of pension eligibility. Again, this is not because annual benefits decline but because the increments under the benefit calculation rules are usually insufficient to compensate for the benefits forgone during the additional years of work. This is equivalent to a pay cut and, as such, can be a significant work disincentive.

In contrast, defined contribution plans are by their very nature age-neutral. They do not decline in value if a worker stays on the job, as the present discounted value of a typical defined benefit plan does. Because of the increasing prevalence of defined contribution plans, another work disincentive late in life has become less important.

Further, Americans are living longer. Life expectancies have increased by three to four years since 1950 and will continue to rise. At age sixty-two, many Americans can anticipate several decades of active involvement, whether in the labor force or other activities. Moreover, the nature of jobs in America is changing. Fewer people

Figure 3.5. Labor Force Participation Rates, Males, Aged 60–64, 1964–2003 (Actual and Fitted Values)

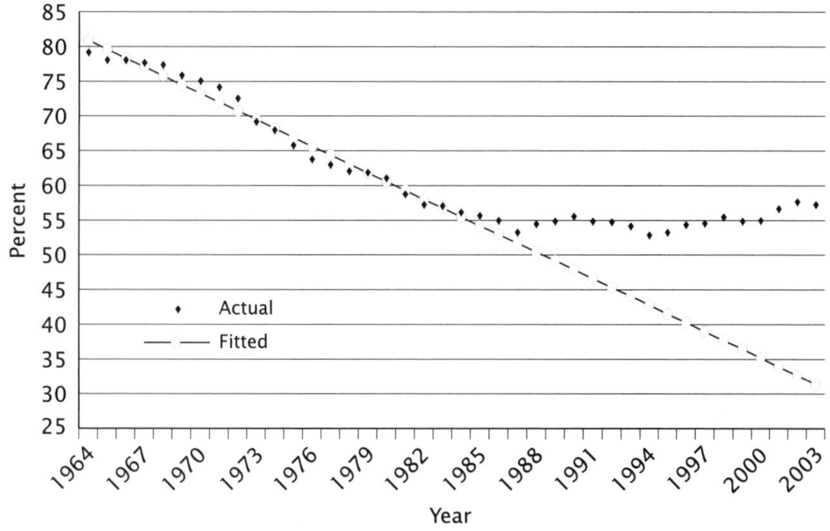

Source: Author's calculations from the Bureau of Labor Statistics Web site, available online at http://stats.bls.gov.

now have physically demanding jobs, which makes continued employment easier for those who want to keep working. There are more service positions and fewer arduous manufacturing jobs.

Finally, technology has been improving and will continue to do so. Many enhancements like computers and hearing aids have made it easier for older workers to stay on the job and have added considerable flexibility about where and when one works.

Given all these changes—cyclical ones like the sustained economic boom and more permanent ones like changes in Social Security and pension incentives or in the occupational structure of the workforce—remaining employed late in life has become a more attractive and even more advisable option for some. What has happened in response to these changes in the retirement environment? Predictably, they have led to important changes in behavior. Older men are not retiring earlier and earlier anymore. In fact, this has not been the case for twenty years. A century-old trend has come to a screeching halt and has even gone into reverse.

In Figures 3.5 and 3.6 (see page 32), the trends for males through the mid-1980s are recapitulated and extrapolated to the present. Then comparison is made between the extrapolation and what actually

Joseph F. Quinn and Teresa Ghilarducci

FIGURE 3.6. LABOR FORCE PARTICIPATION RATES, MALES, AGED 65–69, 1964–2003 (ACTUAL AND FITTED VALUES)

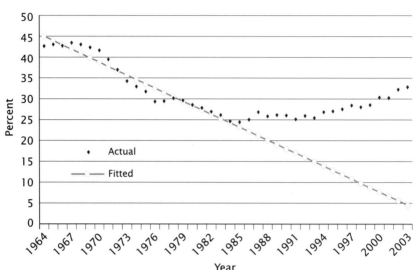

Source: Author's calculations from the Bureau of Labor Statistics Web site, available online at http://stats.bls.gov.

happened to the older male workforce during the past two decades. There has been a striking change in the retirement patterns of men ages sixty to sixty-four and sixty-five to sixty-nine. Similar changes have occurred for men fifty-five to fifty-nine and men seventy and over, though these ranges are not covered in the figures. Men are no longer retiring earlier; on the contrary, in recent years there has been a modest trend toward their increased labor force participation, or delayed retirement.

How have older American women responded to the new calculus of retirement? Although their postwar pattern was very different from that of men—flat rather than declining—nonetheless, since the mid-1980s, as seen in Figures 3.7 and 3.8, the labor force participation of women ages fifty-five to fifty-nine and sixty to sixty-four (and for older women, too, though this is not shown) has broken from the prior trend and increased significantly.

The bottom line is that many more older men and women are working today than prior trends would have predicted. For men, a long-term decline turned flat, then recently increased; for women, a previously stable pattern trend has turned into a dramatic upswing.

Figure 3.7. Labor Force Participation Rates, Females, Aged 55–59, 1964–2003 (Actual and Fitted Values)

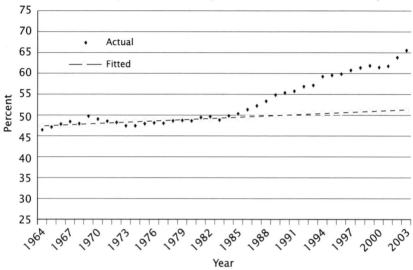

Source: Author's calculations from the Bureau of Labor Statistics Web site, available online at http://stats.bls.gov.

Figure 3.8. Labor Force Participation Rates, Females, Aged 60–64, 1964–2003 (Actual and Fitted Values)

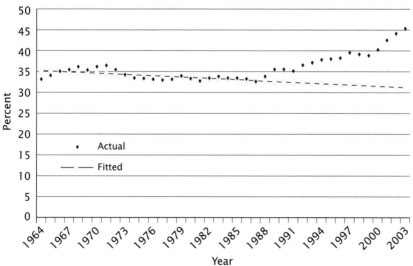

Source: Author's calculations from the Bureau of Labor Statistics Web site, available online at http://stats.bls.gov.

Most of the changes that accompanied these new retirement trends are likely to endure. Mandatory retirement will not return, nor will more generous Social Security early retirement provisions or defined benefit plans, even though some observers would like them to. Longevity and health improvements will continue, as will technological progress that makes working life easier for older people.

Can older workers work longer? Not only can they, they already do. But do people really want to work longer? This answer is a more qualified yes.

Research on how people leave the labor market suggests that many older workers retire gradually, in stages, using bridge jobs between full-time career work and labor force withdrawal. Between a third and a half of older Americans retire in this way, and even that may be an underestimate. Phased retirement is slightly more likely at both ends of the socioeconomic scale: among those who can afford to retire but often choose to keep working and among those who may have no choice but to remain in the labor force.

When older Americans are asked why they keep working, their answers echo this dichotomy. Some say that they want to contribute to society, want to be productive or useful, want to stay mentally and physically active, or enjoy the interactions with their colleagues, all answers that suggest a quality-of-life choice. But many answers emphasize the necessity of work: I need the medical insurance; I have to work to make ends meet. These responses reflect the high degree of income inequality that we tolerate in the United States.

Looking ahead, current trends can be expected to continue. Although the strength of the economy will ebb and flow, the changes in the retirement environment described earlier are here to stay. At the margin, the trade-off between work and leisure facing older Americans has shifted toward work.

When current workers are asked about their plans for late in life, work plays a prominent role. Recent surveys have asked baby boomers if they plan to keep working after retirement or after sixty-five, and the vast majority—between 60 and 80 percent—say yes. Although it is hard to believe that 60 to 80 percent really will work beyond age sixty-five (currently, only a third of men and a fifth of women ages sixty-five to sixty-nine are in the labor force), these survey responses indicate a change in attitude about the appropriate mix of work and leisure late in life. In the new era, retirement is a multistage process, not a single event. Americans will be retiring later than they now do and will combine work, leisure, and other activities as they wind down their participation in the labor force.

There is a vast pool of talented and experienced older workers who are able to work and willing to do so under the right conditions. Recruiting more of them and employing them longer would be good for many of these individuals, good for the firms that are smart enough to hire them, and good for a nation that contemplates the prospect of an aging population.

The authors of a recent Congressional Budget Office study on the retirement prospects of baby boomers conclude that about half of the baby-boomer households are on track to accumulate enough wealth to maintain their working-age standards of living after retirement.[3] That leaves the other half facing a decline in their standard of living if they retire as planned. What better way to avoid this decline than working a few more years? This is a more realistic proposition than expecting that people will save more over their lifetimes, which could accomplish the same goal. Saving enough is difficult to do, particularly if one waits until his or her fifties to try to accumulate sufficient wealth for retirement. In contrast, the decision to work a few more years can be made at the time that retirement is being contemplated rather than forty years earlier. In place of the classic three-legged stool of Social Security, pensions, and personal savings that supported older Americans, there is now a four-legged stool, with the fourth leg being earnings from continued work.

Economists study incentives and how people respond to them. Americans retired earlier and earlier when the incentives induced them to do so, and they stopped retiring earlier and earlier when the incentives were changed. Future retirement patterns—when and how people leave the workforce—are not set in stone. Rather, they will depend on economic and demographic trends in health, life expectancy, technological progress, and the occupational mix, as well as on what with any luck will be enlightened public policy that continues to encourage, or at least not to discourage, labor force participation late in life.

AMERICANS SHOULD NOT BE
REQUIRED TO WORK LONGER

Teresa Ghilarducci

"Can the elderly work longer?" is an absurd question for a rich country. Why not have thirteen-year-olds work, given flextime and job training? Coupling the rhetoric about labor force participation of the elderly with that of child labor highlights that retirement is part of an enduring political debate about which categories of persons are exempted from the imperative to work. Economist John Maynard Keynes predicted economic growth would settle the debate. The fundamental question would be how best to use leisure time when the workday was two hours long.

In his 1928 essay "Economic Possibilities for Our Grandchildren"—baby boomers are the age his grandchildren would be—Keynes wrote, "Let us for the sake of argument suppose that a hundred years from now we are eight times better off per capita in the economic sense than we are today." (The U.S. gross domestic product is now in fact 6.5 times larger than it was in 1928.) He predicted that real economic deprivation would be solved, and "for the first time since his creation man would be forced to confront his real and permanent problem, how to use his freedom from pressing economic cares, how to occupy the leisure, which science and compound interest will have won for him, to live wisely and agreeably and well."[4]

It is a wonder that Keynes could have been so right about many other things and yet could have missed our predicament so thoroughly. Overwork, rather than the problem of living "wisely, agreeably, and well," is arguably the major problem this country confronts. We are debating whether the elderly should work more in a society where the demands of work are increasing and the monetary rewards for work are decreasing.

Earnings growth for most men has not kept up with inflation since the 1970s.[5] Household income has maintained its buying power only because more family members are working and are doing so for longer hours.[6]

It is common knowledge that Americans now work longer than their counterparts in any other industrialized nation. The average figure for hours worked annually in the United States in 1998 was 1,966; the nation with the next highest number was Japan, at 1,889 hours per year, followed by France, the United Kingdom, and Germany. Germans worked just 1,560 hours on average. Only forty years ago, the rankings were quite different. The Germans worked an incredible 2,372 hours per year, the French 1,926, and the Americans a relatively leisurely 1,867, fewer hours than any of the other four nations surveyed here.[7]

If Keynes had lived until 1985 he would have been smug, as there were great gains in leisure for men up to that point. Joseph F. Quinn's findings show that men over age sixty-five experienced a 60 percent decline in labor force participation (which also can be read as a 60 percent gain in leisure) from 1950 to 1985, dropping from an incredible 72 percent labor force participation rate at mid-century. Men over the age of seventy experienced a 70 percent gain in leisure (their labor force participation rate was 50 percent in 1950 and 16 percent in 1985). Also, older women are spending more time working. More women ages sixty-five to seventy are employed now than at any time since 1971. As Quinn says, "A century-old trend has come to a screeching halt. . . ." Americans are working more since 1985 than ever before.

Keynes could have been wrong for one of two reasons: either we Americans actually like work more than Keynes ever imagined we would or leisure lost ground for reasons other than what workers want.

Judging by the available evidence, the latter proposition is truer than the former. The primary reason why older workers are working longer is the decline in retirement income security. The idea that work is becoming more attractive for older workers does not comport with the realities expressed in preference surveys or studies of labor force characteristics.

There are two observations that suggest the elderly, as a rule, value retirement leisure more than work. First, almost all economists' models of retirement behavior that aim to explain the paradoxical phenomenon that people will accept a decrease in income in order to retire when they want conclude that the "taste for leisure increases with age."[8] In addition, directly asking the elderly what they do with their time reinforces the supposition that the value of leisure increases with age. Time-use studies show that the elderly spend more time "dinking around," which takes in the categories of grooming,

watching television, eating, cooking, hobbies, and sports; all are activities that the elderly like better than work.[9]

Countering the formal economic models and time-use studies is
the argument that mental function is enhanced by many aspects of
middle-class work environments. Such work environments may place
demands on cognitive function, provide social support, and create a
personal sense of efficacy.[10] This is especially true for boomers who
are increasingly working in jobs that are less physically demanding
and more mentally challenging. Therefore, this line of thinking runs,
the elderly are working because continuing with a career is associated with maintaining skills and feelings of social utility.

But the evolution of the workplace itself has made it less proba-
ble that the elderly will find work more attractive than retirement.
Precisely because more people identify with their careers and because
work often conveys a sense of mastery, competence, and intrinsic
motivation, the existence of a "gray ceiling"—that is, older employees are less likely to be trained or given new authority or are more
likely to have skills that have depreciated over time —makes employment for older Americans a potential source of denigration.[11]
Marginalization and the sense of insecurity that accompanies it can
develop even if outright discrimination is not an issue.[12]

Work may have negative effects on the health of older people.
Using the Health and Retirement Study of individuals over a ten-year
period, Kevin D. Neuman shows that older men's rate of health
degeneration slows when they retire, and older women actually
improve their health after retirement.[13] His findings suggest that
longevity and retirement trends are linked and that, as the elderly
work more, there could be adverse consequences for both morbidity
and mortality.

WHO LOSES WHEN THE ELDERLY WORK LONGER?

The huge decline in social norms for the length of men's working
lives came about for reasons relating to political economy. Workers
were once "winners" in the political battle over the entitlement to
retire. They garnered pension plans, Social Security improvements,
and a sense of cultural legitimacy for retiring even when a person
was healthy and able to work. Much of the retirement debate was
once about the capacity of the elderly to work. But since the late

FIGURE 3.9. RETIREMENT LEISURE (YEARS TO LIVE MULTIPLIED BY LEISURE PARTICIPATION RATE)

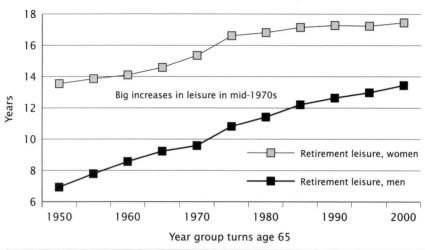

Source: Author's calculations using U.S. Bureau of Labor Statistics data on the labor force participation over time, derived from the Current Population Survey and from mortality tables in Elizabeth Arias, "United States Life Tables, 2002," *National Vital Statistics Reports* 1, no. 3 (2005).

1950s the retirement debate has centered on developing financial security. Therefore, one way to view the data on labor force participation of the elderly is to see victories garnered by American workers in achieving financial support for the privilege of leisure in old age.

Workers have gained, through longer life expectancy, more time spent in retirement. Life expectancy at sixty-five for men in 2000 was 16.3 years, whereas in 1950 it was only 12.8 years. Likewise, female life expectancy at sixty-five increased 22.7 percent, from fifteen years in 1950 to nineteen years in 2000.[14] Up to 1985, as noted, labor force participation rates were dropping, especially for men, but all has changed since then. Putting these trends together tells the entire story. The large gains in leisure came in the mid-1970s, with big increases in Social Security, maturing pension plans, and Medicare taking effect. The number of leisure years each age group could expect to enjoy (the product of multiplying the leisure participation rate, 100 percent minus the labor force participation rate, by the number of years each cohort was expected to live after age sixty-five) burgeoned for both men and women (see Figure 3.9).

The lesson to be learned from Figure 3.9 is that "leisure gains" have not increased since the mid-1980s. Compelling the elderly to work longer to make up for the erosion of retirement income security entails loss of value for senior citizens. Let us not pretend that foul is fair.

Whether harnessing the human resource potential of the elderly represents a win-win situation for workers, employers, and government alike depends mightily on the distribution of economic power between firms and labor. In general, workers have bargaining power when the unemployment rate is decreasing, working conditions have improved, wages are on the rise, and the opportunity cost of not working has diminished. On every count recent evidence suggests that the terms of employment for older workers have tilted against them. Older people are working because they have lost income and because it has become harder to cope with the costs associated with retirement.

Despite the slight decline in unemployment rates in the economic recovery that began in November 2001, the elderly's unemployment rate is mostly increasing. Comparing figures in the recoveries of 1995 and 2002, the unemployment rate for men between the ages of forty-five and sixty rose from 3.5 percent in 1995 to 4.2 percent in 2001; for women it rose from 3.3 to 3.7 percent. Male workers over sixty-five experienced lower rates of unemployment in 2001, dropping to 3.4 percent from 4.3 percent in 1995. But for women in this age group unemployment got worse: 3.7 percent in 1995 and 3.9 percent in 2002.[15]

According to an AARP report on older workers, despite the decline in blue-collar jobs and the improvement in self-reported health conditions overall, there is no evidence that age discrimination has diminished or that the elderly face fewer limitations on their ability to work. There is further no sign that workers are getting the flexible schedules they want or that job satisfaction is high or even rising among the elderly.

To the contrary, older workers enjoy fewer instances of promotions and wage increases. This bias against older workers is even greater in growing industries and occupations where newly educated workers are more desired or where the industry wants a youthful appearance.[16]

According to economic theory, the wages that workers receive are a measure of their value to employers. By this measure, employers' demand for older workers has declined sharply relative to the supply of such workers. Over the past twenty years America has experienced a widening divide between workers with college degrees and those with only a high school education or less. From 1973 to 2001 men who did not have a high school diploma saw the purchasing power of their wages fall by 24 percent. Men with only a high school diploma also suffered a reverse in their real earnings by 11 percent. At the same time, men with advanced degrees enjoyed real earnings gains of 27 percent. Yet, the decline in earnings was much worse for older workers. In fact, only older women with advanced degrees did better after twenty-five years.

The drastic decline in earning power for older workers compared to a generation ago suggests that a welcoming labor market is not the reason the elderly are seeking work. Men ages fifty to sixty-five in 2001 earned from 24 to 37 percent less than their counterparts in 1976. Women fared somewhat better; their decline was not as great as it was for older men, but it was negative (except for those with advanced degrees), whereas for the population as a whole, real wages grew for women at all levels of education (see Table 3.2, page 42).

Baby boomers face declines in pension and Social Security income, and older workers and retirees face large increases in health insurance and health care costs.[17] Because they use more health care resources, older workers cost more to insure than their younger peers. The high costs of older workers and double-digit increases in premiums have caused employers to scale back retiree health benefits. (New accounting rules that require companies' financial statements to reflect their long-term retiree health obligations also contribute to cutbacks.)[18] Older workers effectively experience a pay cut as they shell out more for premiums, and new retirees are experiencing a decline in net retirement income as they are forced to pay more for health benefits. Between 2001 and 2002 total premium costs grew by 16 percent, while the cost borne by new retirees grew by 19 percent.[19] About half of large companies that provide retiree health benefits reported in a 2002 survey that they had already imposed caps on their own contributions, and most of those said they had already reached the cap or expected to do so within the next three years.[20]

The greater difficulty older people face in obtaining health insurance raises the costs of retirement and induces the elderly to work more. With more seniors seeking work or holding onto positions beyond conventional retirement age, employers will be even better situated to dictate the terms of employment.

TABLE 3.2. HOURLY EARNINGS FOR MEN AND WOMEN BY EDUCATION IN 2001 AND PERCENTAGE CHANGE IN REAL EARNINGS (ADJUSTED FOR INFLATION), 1973–2001

Educational attainment	Hourly Earnings in 2001 Dollars		Percentage Change in Real Earnings, 1976–2001		Hourly Earnings in 2001 Dollars		Percentage Change in Real Earnings, 1976–2001	
	Men	Women	Men	Women	Men 50–65	Women 50–65	Men 50–65	Women 50–65
Less than high school	$10.34	$8.21	-24%	0	-11.23	8.56	-28.56	-8.64
High school diploma	$14.37	$11.08	-11%	9%	14.46	10.85	-28.84	-7.82
Some college	$16.48	$12.84	0	17%	16.24	12.6	-31.71	-14.40
College graduate	$25.71	$19.29	15%	27%	18.94	15.92	-37.45	-2.21
Advanced degree	$31.41	$24.35	27%	21%	21.45	23.59	-24.84	19.38

Source: Author's calculations based on Lawrence Mishel, Jared Bernstein, and Heather Boushey, *The State of Working America: 2002–03* (Ithaca, N.Y.: Cornell University Press, 2003), Table 2.17, based on tabulations of data from the Current Population Survey (CPS), 1973 and 2001, for all families; author's calculations based on CPS data for older workers.

DO THE ELDERLY HAVE THE CAPACITY TO WORK LONGER?

One should not easily accept the proposition that the decline in blue-collar work means that the elderly can work more. The debate on the socially optimal retirement age is couched in terms of balancing the economic costs of retirement with workers' ability to perform. Attention has focused chiefly on the cost side of the equation, though. There is no indication that people's disabilities with respect to work have been reduced or that technology changes have made the actual jobs that the elderly are engaged in any easier. Just as many older people say they are unable to work now as did twenty years ago. A full 11.3 percent of those between the ages of fifty-five and sixty-five report they cannot work two years in a row, and that number has been trending upward slightly for twenty years.[21]

WORK-LIMITING HEALTH PROBLEMS AND
CHANCES OF DISPLACEMENT RISE WITH AGE

Work-related disability is defined in government surveys as having a physical or mental condition that limits the kind or amount of work one can do or that prevents one from working altogether. The decline in dependence (the inability to take care of one's self in basic activities of daily living) among the population age sixty-five and older does not necessarily mean that people can be expected to work into their mid- to late sixties or longer. Work-related disability differs from disability in the broader, community sense. The prevalence of disability severe enough to qualify for Social Security disability benefits rises from less than 1 percent of younger workers to about 15 percent of insured workers ages sixty to sixty-four. The impact of a physical problem on one's ability to work varies based on education. Among fifty-five- to sixty-four-year-olds, those with a work disability account for about one in nine college graduates (11 percent); more than one in five of those with only a high school diploma (23 percent); more than one in three high school dropouts (38 percent); and nearly half of those who never entered high school (46 percent).[22]

The risk of disability rises with age, but so does the risk of superannuation (having obsolete skills) and displacement. As work-related disability rises with age, especially for workers with limited education, disability as a consequence of superannuation also becomes prevalent in industries and occupations that are retrenching. Older workers often receive less training, particularly advanced computer training,[23] have less hope for pay increases,[24] and retire earlier from jobs with the worst characteristics.[25] Displaced workers are those who have lost their jobs because their plant or company closed or moved, their positions or shifts were abolished, or their employer did not have enough work for them to do. Workers displaced at older ages are less likely than their younger counterparts to find work. In 1999–2001, four million workers were displaced from jobs they had held for at least three years. Those still without jobs in January 2002 accounted for nearly half (49 percent) of displaced workers ages fifty-five to sixty-four, compared to about one-third (32 percent) of younger displaced workers, those ages twenty-five to fifty-four.[26]

Older displaced workers report that they believe that their age works against them in the job market.[27] According to a fifty-eight-year-old laid-off controller, "There are few ads that say 10-plus years of experience or 15-plus years of experience. If you have more experience than that, it's a presumption that you're over qualified or that they don't want people who are older." An executive recruiter confirmed, "I rarely have someone say, 'Can you find me someone over 50 for this job?' It is almost always, 'Find me someone 35 to 45.'" A laid-off forty-seven-year-old bricklayer observed, "I think they're always looking for younger people. They're stronger, faster. The older you get, you slow down a little bit."[28] Older displaced workers who succeed in finding jobs are more likely than their younger counterparts to experience large earnings losses. One study found that when displaced workers age fifty-five to sixty-four did find full-time, year-round jobs, nearly four in ten experienced a drop in earnings of 20 percent or more.[29] When a group of workers is looking for work in markets where unemployment rates are high, the bargaining leverage resides with the employer.

SHOULD THE ELDERLY WORK MORE?

This country ought not reverse the achievements made in the area of retirement income security. We have a system that distributes retirement leisure fairly well across socioeconomic groups. Employer pensions combined with Social Security early eligibility allows retirement ages to vary so that people can retire at approximately the same "real" age, which is not the same as their chronological age. For healthy, middle-class professionals, sixty-five is "younger" than for people in lower socioeconomic classes because of differing mortality and morbidity rates. Reducing benefits according to birth date penalizes those who age faster. According to a new analysis from the Health and Retirement Study, 11 percent of men and 7 percent of women who retire early die before age sixty-five, largely those who had reported worse health status to begin with. This group is likelier to be poor and nonwhite. Because those who take early retirement tend to die younger, they do not on average enjoy more retirement leisure.[30] Although workers who take early retirement end up with less in the way of Social Security benefits collected over their lifetimes because they typically die earlier—in fact 12 percent less—they would have had 19 percent less in total if they had to wait until age sixty-five to collect Social Security benefits.[31] Even among defined benefit plans, early retirement provisions are invoked more often in industries where labor conditions lead to shorter life spans, thus working to equalize the consumption of leisure among the elderly.[32]

Should the elderly work longer and should they be encouraged to do so by reducing benefits taken at earlier ages are questions about quality of life. Most evidence points to the elderly preferring to retire, but they are working more because of the loss of value in their pensions. The outcome is clearly worse for workers, but it may be good for employers that want to keep wage growth down and that resist labor-saving investments.[33]

Either Keynes was wrong about our fundamental economic problem eventually becoming too much time on our hands because we love work and, in his own words, work is the way we "pluck the hour and the day virtuously," or because his timing was off. Most likely, he was wrong because he could not predict a political economy in which workers would lose retirement income security even as the nation got richer. A more important question to consider than the capabilities of older American workers is, What do we view as optimal for our grandchildren? Will they live to work or work to live?

4.

REMEDIES FOR THE
SAVINGS SHORTFALL

Robert H. Frank

Given the miracle of compound interest, our ability to invest money at even modest rates of return represents an extraordinary opportunity. But it is one that Americans have largely failed to seize. Our savings rate, always low by international standards, has fallen sharply in recent decades. We now save at less than two-thirds the rate we did in the 1970s.[1]

Even more troubling is the large proportion of Americans who save virtually nothing. For example, half of respondents in one national survey reported life savings of less than $3,000. And another 40 percent said that it would be a "big problem" if they had to deal with an unexpected bill for $1,000.[2] A further indication that most middle- and low-income families save too little is that a majority of these families experience significant retrenchments in living standards when they retire.[3]

WHY DO WE SAVE TOO LITTLE?

Although there are numerous contributors to the American savings deficit, the focus here will be on only two. One is that, although people may realize that they would be better off for saving more, they often find it difficult to summon the willpower to do so. A second is that everyone understands that although each would be better off if all saved more, each would be made worse off by a unilateral decision to save more. Savings shortfalls stemming from self-control problems can be remedied by individual action. But those stemming from gaps between individual and social incentives may require collective action.

THE SELF-CONTROL PROBLEM

Some people undoubtedly save too little because they are ill informed about the future consequences of having low incomes during retirement. But even perfectly informed individuals often find immediate consumption opportunities painfully tempting. One might know exactly what is best and yet still have a hard time executing the right choices.[4]

George Ainslie has argued that human and animal nervous systems are simply hardwired to prefer the poorer but more immediate of two goals when it becomes close at hand.[5] Ainslie's hypothesis predicts preference reversals that are widely observed in everyday human behavior. Thus, the dieter vows before dinner to forgo dessert but then has a change of mind when the dessert trolley arrives. That the subsequent expression of regret at having done so is genuine is supported by the fact the dieter deliberately avoids keeping tempting desserts on hand in his or her own kitchen. In the same vein, executives who order their lunches in the morning typically request smaller portions than those who wait until noon.

That saving gets short shrift because of self-control problems is suggested by the enormous costs that many people incur because of their inability to postpone purchases even briefly. The average American family now carries revolving credit card balances that total almost $9,000. Such a family will incur as much as $1,800 a year or more in interest payments. If they had postponed their purchases until they could pay for them out of savings and then used that $1,800 to buy Treasury bonds paying 5 percent interest each year, they would have had an extra $10,443 after five years, an extra $62,494 after twenty years.

DISTORTIONS CAUSED BY CONCERNS
ABOUT RELATIVE CONSUMPTION

Since Adam Smith's time, economists have argued that self-interested persons who trade with one another in competitive markets will be led, as if by an invisible hand, to make the most efficient possible use of society's resources. A key assumption behind this claim is that people derive satisfaction primarily from the absolute quantities of goods and services they consume. Yet, all available evidence from biology, psychology, sociology, and common sense tells us that absolute consumption is not the only, or even the most important, source of human satisfaction. In particular, there is compelling evidence that degree of satisfaction is much better explained by variations in relative consumption levels than by variations in absolute consumption.[6]

If we adopt the biologist's view that human motivations are shaped by natural selection, it is no surprise that people might care so strongly about relative resource holdings. Even in a famine, for example, there is always some food available, and the question of who gets it is settled largely by relative wealth holdings. And in virtually every human society on record, relative wealth holdings have played at least some role in deciding who ends up with the most sought-after marriage partners.[7]

Additional evidence on the importance of relative position comes in the form of happiness surveys conducted over time in a variety of countries. These surveys find that happiness levels within a country at a given moment are strongly positively correlated with a respondent's position in the country's income distribution. The same studies find no long-term trends in average reported happiness levels, even for countries whose incomes have been growing steadily over time.

These survey findings are consistent with the view that relative position on the income scale is a much more important determinant of self-assessed happiness levels than is one's absolute measure of prosperity. Even though happiness surveys call for purely subjective responses, the phenomenon that they measure is real. Numerous other studies have found strong positive relationships between reported happiness levels and observable physiological and behavioral measures of well-being.[8]

In his 1949 book *Income, Saving, and the Theory of Consumer Behavior,* James Duesenberry suggested that concerns about relative living standards help explain why people save too little. People who find themselves mixing with others with higher material living standards inevitably experience a sense of relative deprivation, which they attempt to escape by saving less and spending more.

Many economists, however, view this explanation as problematic because saving less now means experiencing even greater relative deprivation in the future. This objection may help to explain why most intermediate macroeconomics textbooks no longer even mention Duesenberry's relative income hypothesis. It is of course true that lower savings today usually means lower spending in the future. Yet, concerns about current relative living standards may nonetheless reduce current savings if they operate with greater force than concerns about future relative consumption. Such a differential appears plausible for at least three reasons.

One is the general human tendency toward myopia mentioned earlier. Although the consequences of current relative living standards are immediate and vivid, those of future relative living standards can only be imagined. The press of daily business keeps most of us from thinking about our future circumstances very often, and evidence suggests that our attempts to imagine them are often wildly optimistic. More than 40 percent of survey respondents, for example, say they believe their heirs will pay estate taxes, when in fact only about 1 percent of estates will be affected by this tax.[9]

A second reason that concerns about current relative consumption might affect savings is that many important outcomes depend much more on current than future relative consumption. Although most parents want to send their children to the best schools possible and also to save enough to support a comfortable standard of living in retirement, these goals are squarely in conflict. Parents can spend more now for a house in a better school district, or they can save more now for retirement. Most view the more immediate goal as more important.

The problem is that a "good school" is an inescapably relative concept. It is a school that is better than most others. In the United States, where school budgets are funded largely by real estate taxes, school quality tends to track local house prices closely. To send one's children to an above-average school, one must thus buy a house that exceeds the median home price in the area. Families may know full well that stretching their budgets to finance such a house will entail an unpleasantly low living standard during retirement. But the desire to avoid sending their children to a (relatively) low-quality school in a neighborhood perhaps considered unsafe trumps that worry. Most parents opt for the better school now and hope for the best when it comes time to retire.

The aggregate effects of such choices, however, often turn out to be far from what people intend. Thus, when everyone spends more on a house in a better school district, the result is merely to bid up the prices of those houses. In the process, no one moves forward in the educational hierarchy, and yet, parents end up having smaller savings for retirement. Acting as individuals, however, they have no real alternative except to send their children to less desirable schools.

A third reason for placing disproportionate weight on current living standards is that people who consume more now may actually enhance their future income prospects. Job seekers, for example, are told they should "look good" for interviews. Like a good education, however, tasteful appearance is a relative concept. To look good means simply to look better than others who want the same job you do. The most direct means to this end is to spend more than they do on clothing. The catch is that this same calculus operates for everyone. The result is a fruitless escalation in the amount people have to spend merely to appear presentable. From a collective perspective, it would make sense to save more and spend less on clothing. But it would not pay any individual, acting alone, to take this step.

Duesenberry's relative income hypothesis works as long as concerns about current relative living standards exert greater force on behavior than concerns about future relative living standards. And it has long been clear that the relative income hypothesis does a better job than competing theories of explaining important patterns in the savings data.[10]

Duesenberry's relative income hypothesis also suggests why middle-income families in the United States save much less now than in the 1970s. According to competing theories, changes in income inequality will have no effect on how much a family with a given income spends. By contrast, the relative income hypothesis predicts that a family will spend more if its relative position in the income distribution declines.

Recent changes in the distribution of income in the United States provide an opportunity to put these conflicting predictions to the

FIGURE 4.1. CHANGES IN BEFORE-TAX HOUSEHOLD INCOMES, 1949–1979

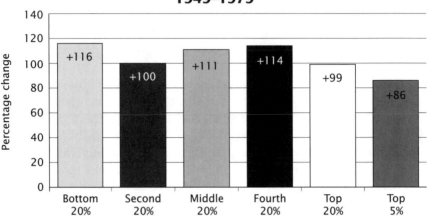

Source: Author's calculations.

test. During the three decades following World War II, incomes grew at about the same rate for families up and down the income ladder. Since then, however, most of the economic gains have been captured by families near the top (see Figures 4.1 and 4.2).

Income inequality also has increased in two important ways not portrayed in Figures 4.1 and 4.2. One is that changes in the income tax structure during the Reagan and George W. Bush presidencies significantly shifted real, after-tax purchasing power in favor of those atop the socioeconomic ladder. Another is that the magnitude of the earnings gains recorded by those at the very top has been almost without historical precedent. According to *Business Week*'s annual compensation survey, CEOs of the largest U.S. companies earned more than five hundred times as much as the average worker in 2001, compared to just forty-two times as much in 1980. Available data for top earners suggest that similar changes have occurred in other market segments.[11]

According to prevailing theories of consumption, which assume that an individual's satisfaction depends only on his or her own absolute consumption, the observed distributional changes predict substantial increases in consumption by top earners and little or no change in consumption by those in the middle. These theories also suggest that the observed changes in income patterns have not been costly for middle-class families.

Figure 4.2. Changes in Before-Tax Incomes, 1979–1999

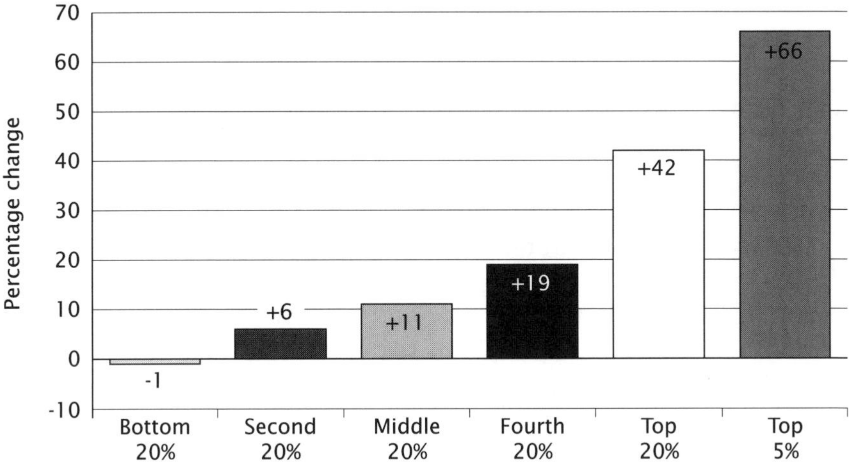

Source: Author's calculations.

Indeed, such families not only appear untroubled by extensive media coverage of the lifestyles of the rich and famous, they also actually find it entertaining. Sociological studies consistently confirm that the comparisons that really matter are highly local in character.[12] As Bertrand Russell once remarked, "Beggars don't envy millionaires; they envy other beggars who earn more than they do."

But even if local comparisons are the only ones that count, sharply increased spending by top earners may nonetheless have spawned increased feelings of relative deprivation among the middle class. When top earners build larger mansions, for example, they shift the frame of reference that defines an acceptable house for those just slightly below them on the income scale. And when those people respond by building bigger houses, they in turn shift the frame of reference for those just below them, and so on, all the way down the scale.

Increased expenditures by top earners may thus launch an "expenditure cascade" that results in increased expenditures even among those whose incomes have not risen. With respect to housing, the single most important category of household expenditure, the cascade hypothesis tracks experience far more closely than conventional consumption models. Thus, the median size of a newly constructed house in the United States, which stood at less than 1,600 square feet in 1980, had risen above 2,100 square feet by 2001, despite the fact that the median family's real income had increased only slightly in the intervening years.[13]

Many economists appear reluctant to introduce concerns about relative consumption into public policy decisions, perhaps for fear that doing so would encourage people to give freer rein to envy and other destructive emotions. But the observed changes in income inequality have important implications for the spending decisions of even those families who are completely unconcerned about relative house size per se. As noted earlier, the difficulty confronting such families is that buying a cheaper than average house typically entails sending their children to schools of below-average quality. So one need not invoke envy to explain why they might feel compelled to keep pace with others' expenditures on housing.

A similar logic applies to a middle-class family's decision about which car to purchase, for in this domain as well, there is evidence of an expenditure cascade. Higher incomes at the top have induced top earners to buy cars that are faster, more luxuriously appointed, and heavier than those purchased by their counterparts two decades earlier. But the same changes characterize automobiles marketed directly to middle-income consumers whose incomes have risen little. Today's entry-level Honda Civic is, at 2,500 pounds, about the same size as 1985's Honda Accord, whose current model weighs 3,200 pounds. For about the same real price, an Accord buyer in 1985 could buy today's Civic and in the process do better on virtually every performance dimension. The new Civic is faster and more reliable than the old Accord. It has nicer upholstery and a better sound system. It even gets better gas mileage.

But people who buy a 2,500-pound Civic today will incur a significant risk that they would not have in their 1985 Accords because they must now share the roads with 6,000-pound Lincoln Navigators and 7,500-pound Ford Excursions. The odds of being killed in a collision rise roughly fivefold if a smaller car is struck by one of these large vehicles. To explain why many families might decide against today's Honda Civic, again one need not assume that they are driven by envy or other psychological frailties.

How can middle-class families be spending significantly more on housing, cars, clothing, gifts, and other goods if median earnings are only slightly higher than in the late 1970s? The answer is that they appear to be working every margin. They are saving less, borrowing more, working longer hours, commuting longer distances,

TABLE 4.1. THE EFFECT OF EARNINGS
INEQUALITY ON MEDIAN HOUSE PRICES

Independent Variable	Coefficient	Standard Error	T-Ratio	P
Constant	-71,968.0	33,974	-2.12	0.0356
% Retired	-1,570.12	437.8	-3.59	0.0004
Median income	3.08256	0.3418	9.02	<0.0001
Inequality (95/50)	38,222.3	6568	5.82	<0.0001
Expenditure per pupil	-0.7673	1.220	-0.63	0.5302

Sample: 181 U.S. school districts in 2000.

Dependent variable: Median house price ($)

Source: Author's calculations.

and filing for personal bankruptcy at much higher rates than their counterparts in the 1970s and 1980s.[14]

Is there any evidence that the growth in income inequality of recent decades has played a causal role in the expenditure cascades described above? Bjornulf Ostvik-White, Adam Levine, and I have attempted to answer this question using census figures on earnings inequality and a variety of data on expenditure and financial distress.[15] Our principal focus was on housing, which is by far the most important expenditure category for middle-income consumers.

Using data specially prepared by the Census Bureau, we regressed median house prices in the year 2000 for a random sample of 181 U.S. school districts against income inequality (as measured by the ratio of the 95th percentile family's earnings to the median family's earnings in each district) and a selection of control variables, including median income, percentage of persons retired, and per pupil school expenditures. For most of the school districts in our sample, the 95/50 ratio varied from 2.0 to 6.0, with only a handful of districts outside that range. Median house prices in the sample averaged just a bit less than $125,000. The results of this regression are reported in Table 4.1.

We found that median house prices rose slightly more than three dollars for each dollar increase in median income, a link that is broadly consistent with the financial rule of thumb that one should expect to pay roughly three times one's annual income for a home. The expectation that median house prices would be lower in districts heavily populated by retirees was confirmed by our estimate that each one-point increase in the percentage of persons retired yielded a price decline of almost $1,600. Public school expenditure per pupil was included as an additional control variable to allow for the possibility that houses in better school districts might command premium prices.[16]

For the purposes of this volume, of course, the coefficient of greatest interest is the one associated with the measure used to represent income inequality. By almost any standard it is unusually large: each unit increase in the 95/50 ratio was associated with an increase in median house price of more than $38,000. That median house prices will be higher in school districts displaying more severe inequality is predicted by the expenditure cascade hypothesis. Our data emphatically confirm this prediction. In contrast, conventional consumption models predict no link between median house prices and income inequality.

Table 4.2 helps illustrate the scale of the effect by examining some of the relevant characteristics of two Midwestern towns, Danville, Indiana, and Mount Vernon, Illinois. The two have almost the same percentage of retired persons, so their median house prices should not differ significantly on that account. But because median income in the year 2000 was more than $10,000 lower in Danville than in Mount Vernon, the home-financing rule of thumb predicts a median house price in Mount Vernon roughly $30,000 higher than in Danville.

Yet the median house price in Danville, at almost $131,000, was actually more than twice as large as the corresponding median in Mount Vernon. According to the expenditure cascade hypothesis, this reversal is in part a consequence of Danville's 95/50 ratio being more than twice the corresponding ratio in Mount Vernon in the year 2000. The median family in Danville had to make its way in an environment shaped in part by the spending of a family at the 95th percentile earning more than $141,000 a year. In contrast, the 95th percentile family in Mount Vernon earned just in excess of $83,000. At face value, these estimates suggest that the costs imposed on middle-income families by rising income inequality may be high indeed.

There is additional evidence in support of the expenditure cascade hypothesis. Ostvik-White, Levine, and I found that states with higher 95/50 ratios also have significantly higher personal bankruptcy rates,

TABLE 4.2. HOUSE PRICES IN TWO MIDWESTERN TOWNS

	Danville, IN	Mount Vernon, IL
Median income	$30,680	$40,893
Percentage retired	30.5%	30.9%
Median house price	$130,900	$62,280
95/50 ratio	4.62	2.043

Source: Author's calculations.

divorce rates, and average commute times.[17] Using OECD data across countries and over time, Samuel Bowles and Yongjin Park found that total hours worked were positively associated with higher inequality, as measured by both the 95/50 ratio and the Gini coefficient.[18]

In sum, available evidence suggests that rising inequality imposes not only psychological stresses on the members of middle-income families but also a host of other, more tangible economic costs. A family's ability to achieve a variety of important objectives in life depends not just on how much it spends in absolute terms but also on how its expenditures compare with those of others. This pressure to succeed creates expenditure "arms races" that crowd out savings. Families could achieve preferred outcomes if all saved at a higher rate. But, as in a military arms race, a family that saved more unilaterally would often end up faring worse.

POLICY REMEDIES

Americans appear to save too little both because of self-control problems and because of social dilemmas stemming from concern about relative consumption. Unsurprisingly, policies designed to attack one problem will not necessarily provide effective remedies for the other.

Policies for avoiding temptation: opt-out paternalism. If self-control problems caused everyone to save too little, voters might support laws requiring them to save at higher rates. But many are not prone to self-control problems, and such people often have no wish to save

more. So it is natural to ask whether people with self-control problems can overcome them in some way that does not entail restricting
others.

At first glance, such remedies seem readily available. People can
enroll in 401(k) and other similar savings plans that automatically
divert a portion of their earnings into savings accounts that cannot be
accessed without penalty until retirement. If self-control is the problem, keeping one's money out of easy reach seems like an ideal solution.

As a practical matter, however, many people do not participate
even when 401(k) plans are known to be available. Richard Thaler,
David Laibson, and others argue that failure to take the active step of
enrolling in a 401(k) plan is more often the result of inertia or pro-
crastination than of a purposeful decision not to participate.[19] They
note that by simply changing the default option from nonparticipation
to participation, the fraction of employees who sign up often leaps
spectacularly. James J. Choi and colleagues report that, for a sample
of firms in which participation rates varied between 26 percent and 69
percent when an active decision to participate was required, rates
rose to 85 percent when participation was made the default option.

Some might object that setting participation in 401(k) and other
similar savings plans as the default option constitutes paternalism,
but if so it is paternalism with a light touch. These "opt-out" forms
of paternalism are not perfect. If the default contribution rate (percentage of income saved) were set too high, the natural inertia of
decisionmakers could result in excessive savings. Conversely, if the
default contribution rate were set too low, it might actually reduce
aggregate savings in the long run. As noted, the current savings rate
in the United States is too low by any reasonable standard.
Accordingly, if participation in 401(k) plans were made the default
option, most people would probably fare better than under current
arrangements, even if the default savings rate were set well above the
current one.

Policies for solving the collective action problem. To the extent that
our national savings shortfall results not from self-control problems
but from competitive consumption, opt-out paternalism will not be an
effective remedy. Suppose that families save too little because they
use all available funds to bid against one another for houses in the
best school districts. Making participation in 401(k) plans the default

option with a 15 percent savings rate would not slow this bidding war for long. By opting out of the savings plan, a family could free up cash to support a bigger mortgage and thereby send its children to a better school. Other families would inevitably follow suit, and as more families did so the pressures on remaining families to opt out would increase still further.

One escape from this quandary would be a legal requirement that each family save at least a threshold fraction of its earnings each year. In one sense, the Social Security program is just such a requirement. The payroll tax in effect renders 15 percent of gross labor earnings unavailable for the bidding war for a house in a better school district. Of course, Social Security is not a savings program at all but rather a transfer from workers to retirees. But from the perspective of any individual, it is the functional equivalent of a savings plan.

Proposals have surfaced in recent years to transform Social Security from a pay-as-you-go system to a genuine savings program. Doing so would take advantage of the miracle of compound interest, an opportunity that the current system completely misses. Debate on these proposals usually stalls over the question of how to fund them. Calls to increase the payroll tax, which is highly regressive, draw immediate objections on equity grounds. Proposals to raise top marginal tax rates on income would sidestep these objections. But, citing concerns about higher top rates acting as a disincentive to save and invest, legislators now seem more inclined to reduce those rates than to increase them. Absent a new source of general revenue (more on which in a moment), it is not clear how the government could fund a new program of individual savings accounts.

Mandating higher savings is a form of intervention that recalls the heavy-handed, command-and-control regulations employed in the early years of the battle against environmental pollution. There is too much pollution simply because polluting is more attractive to individual firms than to society as a whole. The most efficient way to attack the problem, economists argued, was to levy charges on those whose activities generate pollution. Recent experience has shown that effluent taxes and permit fees have enabled pollution to be curbed at only a fraction of the cost formerly incurred under prescriptive regulation.

Similarly, if the problem at hand is that certain forms of private consumption currently seem more attractive to individuals than to society as a whole, the simplest solution is to make them less attractive by taxing them. Shifting to a progressive consumption tax could restructure incentives in just this way.

Proposals to tax consumption raise the specter of forbidding complexity—of having to save receipts for each purchase, of endless bickering over which products are to be exempt, and so on. Yet, a system of progressive consumption taxation could be achieved by a simple, one-line amendment to the federal tax code, namely, making savings exempt from tax. This is so because the amount a family consumes each year is just the difference between the amount it earns and the amount it saves. Administratively, a progressive consumption tax is thus essentially similar to our current progressive income tax.

The following example illustrates how a progressive consumption tax might work for a family of four if the standard deduction were $7,500 per person. With a total standard deduction of $30,000 per year, the family's taxable consumption would be calculated as its income minus $30,000 minus its savings minus its income tax. A family whose income was no more than $30,000 plus the amount it saved would owe no tax at all under this plan. Because high-income families save a substantially higher proportion of their incomes than low-income families, maintaining the current tax burden across income levels would require top marginal tax rates on consumption that are much steeper than the current top marginal tax rates on income. In the illustrative rate schedule shown in Table 4.3, families with positive taxable consumption are taxed at an initial rate of 20 percent, which then rises gradually as taxable consumption increases.

The top rate of 200 percent shown in the table means that someone who was already spending more than $4 million per year would need three dollars of additional income to support each additional dollar of consumption. Given this rate schedule, Table 4.4 (see page 62) shows how much tax families with different income and savings levels would pay.

The progressive consumption tax illustrated above is different from other consumption taxes like the value-added tax or the national sales tax, which are levied at the same rate no matter how much a family consumes. Those taxes have been criticized as regressive because of the strong correlation between savings rates and household income. Under the tax proposed here, escalating marginal tax rates on consumption, coupled with the large standard deduction, ensure that total tax as a proportion of income rises steadily with income, even though the assumed savings rate is sharply higher for high-income families.

TABLE 4.3. TAX RATES ON TAXABLE CONSUMPTION

Taxable Consumption	Marginal Tax Rate
0–$39,999	20 percent
$40,000–$49,999	22 percent
$50,000–$59,999	24 percent
$60,000–$69,999	26 percent
$70,000–$79,999	28 percent
$80,000–$89,999	30 percent
$90,000–$99,999	32 percent
$100,000–$129,999	34 percent
$130,000–$159,999	38 percent
$160,000–$189,999	42 percent
$190,000–$219,999	46 percent
$220,000–$249,999	50 percent
$250,000–$499,000	60 percent
$500,000–$999,999	80 percent
$1,000,000–$1,999,999	100 percent
$2,000,00–$3,999,999	150 percent
$4,000,000+	200 percent

Source: Author's calculations.

Consumption taxation has been proposed before.[20] But although some proponents have argued that it will encourage savings, many economists insist that it will not because it does not affect the price of current consumption relative to that of future consumption.[21] These critics concede the tax makes current consumption more expensive but argue that, because it also raises the price of future consumption by the same margin, it provides no reason to postpone current consumption.

This objection has force. But even though the proposed tax does not alter the price of current relative to future consumption, it does alter other important relative prices that influence the savings decision. In particular, it lowers the marginal costs of self-insuring and inheritance. Although traditional economic theories suggest that people consume most or all of their earnings before they die, many in fact leave estates whose magnitudes are far larger than could reasonably be attributed to uncertainty regarding the time of death. People leave

TABLE 4.4. ILLUSTRATIVE INCOME, SAVINGS, AND TAX VALUES UNDER A PROGRESSIVE CONSUMPTION TAX

Income	Savings	Taxable Consumption	Tax
$30,000	$1,500	0	0
$50,000	$3,000	$14,167	$2,833
$100,000	$10,000	$49,836	$10,164
$150,000	$20,000	$81,538	$18,462
$200,000	$40,000	$104,328	$25,672
$500,000	$120,000	$258,000	$92,000
$1,000,000	$300,000	$458,000	$212,000
$1,500,000	$470,000	$646,000	$354,000
$2,500,000	$800,000	$1,029,900	$667,100
$3,500,000	$1,200,000	$1,316,400	$953,600
$20,000,000	$10,000,000	$4,444,267	$5,525,733

Source: Author's calculations.

estates for many different reasons, but two in particular stand out. One is to hedge against the possibility that becoming disabled would rob them of their earning power. Another is to leave bequests to heirs and charities. Various market imperfections make private savings more attractive than commercial insurance as a hedge against lost earning power. A steeply progressive consumption tax reduces the cost of self-insuring. And it lowers the cost of providing for heirs and charities. On both accounts, the progressive consumption tax can be expected to stimulate higher savings.

A separate channel through which such a tax would limit current consumption is direct constraint of the expenditures of affluent individuals who now consume most or all of their after-tax incomes. Consider a person who currently earns $3.5 million a year and consumes all the after-tax income (say, $2,100,000 per year). Under the illustrative tax whose rates are shown in Table 4.3, the most this person could consume and still cover his or her tax bill out of current income would be $1,733,120, a reduction of more than 17 percent.

If the tax affected spending directly, either through its impact on the relative prices of self-insuring against income losses and of leaving bequests or through the constraints it imposes on high spenders, it also would affect spending indirectly. Each individual's spending, after all, constitutes part of the frame of reference that influences what others spend. Given the apparent strength of relative income in swaying spending patterns, the indirect effects of a progressive consumption tax promise to be considerably larger than the direct effects.

Switching to a progressive consumption tax would create a revenue source for funding equity accounts to supplement Social Security payments during retirement as well. For, unlike higher top marginal rates on income, higher top marginal rates on consumption would not limit incentives to save and invest; rather, they would actually encourage thrift.

WOULD A CONSUMPTION TAX
CAUSE UNEMPLOYMENT?

It might seem natural to worry that a tax that limits consumption could lead to recession and unemployment. This is not a serious long-run concern, however, because money that is not spent on consumption would be saved and invested. The result is that some of the people who are now employed to produce consumption goods would instead be employed to produce capital goods, which, in the long run, would increase the economy's productive capacity.

As for the short run, if a recession should occur, a more powerful fiscal remedy would be available under a consumption tax than is currently available under the income tax. Under the current tax structure, a standard textbook remedy for recession is a temporary income tax cut. The problem with this, however, is that those who remain employed have a strong incentive to save the money attributable to tax cuts as a hedge against the possibility of becoming unemployed. A temporary consumption tax cut would avoid this difficulty since the only way consumers could benefit from it would be by actually spending more money now. Transition problems could be minimized by introducing the program gradually—with phased increases in the amount of savings a family could exempt and phased hikes in the highest marginal tax rates.

CONCLUDING REMARKS

With the average family currently carrying almost $9,000 in unpaid credit card balances, it is difficult to second-guess the claim that Americans save too little. Evidence suggests that we do so in part because we find many consumption opportunities irresistibly tempting and in part because we face pressure to keep pace with escalating community consumption standards.

In principle, individuals can shield themselves from the temptation to spend too much by enrolling in payroll deduction savings plans that place a portion of their earnings out of easy reach. Simple inertia appears to prevent many people from taking this step. Evidence from several studies suggests that people would be more likely to achieve their individual savings goals if participation in 401(k) and other employer savings plans were made the default option.

Savings shortfalls that stem from consumption "arms races" yield less readily to solution. Curbing such arms races is likely to require either mandating higher savings directly (as by funding individual retirement savings accounts out of general tax revenues) or else rewarding higher savings by substantially increasing the price of current consumption (as by switching to a progressive consumption tax). Such policies clearly do constrain individual behavior (indeed, that is their aim). Yet, even a steeply progressive consumption tax is not an especially intrusive measure. After all, the government must tax something; across-the-board reductions in consumption do not appear to entail significant losses in terms of middle- and upper-income citizens' sense of satisfaction, and these are the only people who might experience a heavier tax burden under a progressive levy on spending.

5.

PENSION REFORM IN SWEDEN

Annika Sundén

INTRODUCTION

Population aging has put increasing pressures on public pension systems around the world. As a result, many countries are discussing how to reform their public pension systems in order to meet the demands of an aging society and preserve fiscal balance. A trend in the reforms that have already taken place is the shift from defined benefit plans to defined contribution plans. Compared to defined benefit plans, defined contribution plans place more of the risk and responsibility to plan for retirement on individuals.

Sweden was an early mover in the reform process. It is interesting to look at Sweden because the reform that was implemented fundamentally changed its public pension system. Furthermore, it recognized that pension systems are dynamic institutions and incorporated automatic adjustments to ensure financial stability. The Swedish reform therefore provides some important lessons for other countries.

In 1994, the Swedish parliament passed legislation that transformed the nation's public pension system from a pay-as-you-go, defined benefit plan to a Notional Defined Contribution plan (NDC).

In addition, the reform introduced a second tier of funded benefits. The 1994 decision was taken in principle, and many issues remained to be solved. Between 1994 and the spring of 1998 the details of the reform were worked out, and the proposal was written into law. The reformed pension system went into effect in 1999. An important goal of the Swedish reform was to design a system that was fiscally as well as politically sustainable in the long run. In particular, the reformers wanted to create a system in which adjustments to maintain financial stability were made automatically. They concluded that it was possible to achieve this goal only by overhauling the system rather than changing its parameters.

THE NEED FOR REFORM

In the mid-1980s, actuarial projections began to show that the Swedish public pension system would eventually face considerable financial shortfalls. Several characteristics contributed to the troubles: the system was sensitive to economic growth because it was indexed to prices rather than wages; the population was aging; and the maturity of the system was placing increasing pressures on it because benefit levels were increasing. The benefit formula implied an inequitable and unsystematic relationship between benefits and contributions.

The prereform public pension system in Sweden combined a flat-rate universal benefit (Folkpension, or FP) with an earnings-related benefit (Allmän Tjänstepension, or ATP). The ATP system had been introduced in 1960, and the FP benefit went back as far as 1913. The ATP was based on an individual's fifteen years of highest earnings, required thirty years of covered earnings for a full pension, and replaced 60 percent of earnings up to a ceiling. Individuals with no or very low ATP benefits received an additional benefit, the pension supplement, which was equivalent to about 50 percent of the FP benefit. Earned pension rights and benefits as well as the system's ceiling on benefits were indexed to prices.

The FP and ATP benefits were financed primarily through payroll taxes levied on the employer. The system was pay-as-you-go with partial funding. The payroll taxes for the FP and ATP systems were 5.86 percent and 13 percent respectively in 1997, so that the total

TABLE 5.1. OLD-AGE PENSION SPENDING IN EIGHT COUNTRIES IN 2000 AND PROJECTED CHANGE, 2000–2050

	Percentage of GDP in 2000	Projected Change 2000–2050 (percentage points)
Canada	5.1	5.8
Germany	11.8	5.0
Italy	14.2	-0.3
Japan	7.9	0.6
Netherlands	6.4	4.8
Sweden	11.1	1.6
United Kingdom	4.3	-0.7
United States	4.4	1.8

Source: Ageing and Income: Financial Resources and Retirement in Nine OECD Countries, Organization for Economic Cooperation and Development, Paris, 2001.

contribution rate was close to 19 percent. The financing for the FP benefit was supplemented by general tax revenues. When the system was introduced in 1960, the contribution rate was set so that a surplus would build up. This was done to create a demographic buffer and to offset an expected decrease in personal saving following the introduction of a universal, earnings-related benefit. The surplus was funneled into a set of buffer funds that initially were equal to approximately five years' worth of benefits.

In addition to the public system, almost all workers in Sweden receive benefits from occupational pensions. On average these plans replace an additional 10 percent of earnings.[1]

Before discussing the reform process, it is useful to contrast expenditures on old-age pensions and demographic developments in Sweden with those of some other countries to get a sense of the magnitude of the problem. The Swedish public pension system is sizable, and public expenditures on old-age pensions amounted to 11.1 percent of GDP in 2000 (see Table 5.1). This compared to 4.4 percent of GDP in the United States and 4.3 percent in the United Kingdom.

Public expenditure is projected to increase in almost all of the advanced industrial countries between 2000 and 2050, with the

**TABLE 5.2. SHARE OF POPULATION AGED 65 AND OVER AND
DEPENDENCY RATIO IN EIGHT COUNTRIES, 2000 AND 2030**

	Share of Population Aged 65 and Over (percent)		Dependency Ratio: Ratio of Population Aged 65 and Over to Population 16–64 (percent)	
	2000	*2030*	*2000*	*2030*
Canada	12.8	22.6	18.7	37.3
Germany	16.4	26.1	24.0	43.3
Italy	18.2	29.1	26.9	49.1
Japan	17.1	27.3	25.0	46.0
Netherlands	13.8	25.6	20.2	43.0
Sweden	17.4	25.5	27.1	43.4
United Kingdom	16.0	23.1	24.6	38.3
United States	12.5	20.6	19.0	33.6

*Source: Ageing and Income: Financial Resources and Retirement in Nine OECD
Countries,* Organization for Economic Cooperation and Development, Paris,
2001.

largest increases in Canada and Germany; most of the increase can be
explained by population aging.[2] By the time of the reform, Sweden
was already beginning to take on the characteristics of an aging society. In 2000, 17.4 percent of the population in Sweden was over sixty-
five, while in the United States the comparable proportion was 12.5
percent (see Table 5.2). By 2030, these respective shares are estimated to increase to 25.5 percent and 20.5 percent. Overall, population
aging is less severe in North America than in Europe and Japan largely because of greater immigration. In 2003 the dependency ratio is
estimated to be 33.6 percent in the United States, as opposed to 43.3
percent in Sweden and 46 percent in Japan.

The combination of the generous pension system and population aging made the Swedish problem severe. At the time of the
reform, projections showed that with future real wage growth of 1.5
percent and unchanged contribution rates, the buffer funds would
be exhausted sometime between 2010 and 2015. In order to maintain fiscal stability, total contribution rates would have to be boost-
ed to about 24 percent by 2015 and would need to increase further

subsequently. In fact, projections showed that the system would be sustainable only at future real wage growth of 2 percent, and then merely because an increasing share of workers would have earned pensions above the ceiling and therefore they would not collect. In the United States, by contrast, the 2003 Social Security trustees' report showed that the projected long-term financial deficit was 1.92 percent of taxable payroll in 2002, and the combined Old-Age and Survivors Insurance and Disability Insurance trust funds were projected to be exhausted by 2042.[3]

Public trust in the pension system also was eroding in Sweden. The view that the system would not be able to meet its promises had started to become widespread, in particular among young entrants to the labor force.[4]

THE REFORM PROCESS

By the early 1990s it was clear something had to be done with the Swedish pension system. The government had appointed a commission to study the pension system in 1984. The commission completed its report in 1990 and concluded that the Swedish pension system was bound to run into serious financial difficulties around 2020. It proposed dealing with the long-term deficit by indexing the system to economic growth instead of consumer prices and increasing the normal retirement age as well as the number of years of work required for a full pension. In elections in 1991 the Social Democratic Party was defeated and replaced by a four-party liberal/conservative coalition government. Pension reform became a top priority, and the new government appointed a special group to consider the issue, with representatives of all seven parties then in the parliament. The group, which was headed by the minister for social policy, was organized along unconventional lines for a Swedish commission. Membership was confined to the parliamentarians; no representatives of labor market organizations or retired peoples' associations were included.[5]

The group began with a thorough analysis of the pension system and extended the projections done by the original pension commission. It reached a broad agreement on the problems with the old pension system:

- Sensitive to economic growth. Pension benefits as well as earned pension rights were indexed to prices rather than wages. The absence of a link between benefits and the real wage growth of the working population imperiled the system's solvency in times of low or negative productivity growth. Projections done in the early 1990s indicated that with real wage growth of 1.5 percent and unchanged rules, payroll taxes would need to be 30 percent of wages in 2025 in order for the system to meet its obligations.

- Vulnerable to demographic change. Like other industrialized countries, Sweden is experiencing a rise in the average age of its population. As a result, the number of individuals between twenty and sixty-four relative to the number of individuals sixty-five and older will decrease from 3.2 percent in the early 1990s to 2.4 in 2025.

- The principle of compensation for work effort had eroded. Only income up to a ceiling counted toward pension rights. Because the ceiling was indexed to follow consumer prices, real wage growth meant that successively larger proportions of the population earned wages above the ceiling, eroding income replacement under the ATP arrangement.

- The connection between contributions and benefits was tenuous. Contributions were paid on all earnings from age sixteen until retirement, while benefits were based only on the fifteen years with highest earnings. Thus, the formula redistributed income from those with long working lives and relatively flat earnings growth across the life cycle (typically low-income workers) to those with shorter work histories and rising earnings profiles (typically high-income workers).

- Labor market distortions. The way the benefit formula was applied, considering the payment of contributions on all earnings, reduced incentives for labor force participation.

- Weak incentives to save. Studies suggested that the pay-as-you-go pension system had a negative effect on the national saving rate, even though the system was only partially funded.[6]

The pension group considered several alternatives for reform. One suggestion was to make changes along the lines proposed by the original pension commission. This path was rejected because the group concluded that it would constitute just a temporary fix and would not resolve uncertainty about the system; one important objective was to have a system that was robust and resistant to political risk. The conservative parties argued for a funded and privatized setup, but this was rejected by the Social Democrats, who strongly argued to keep the system public and pay-as-you-go. Because an important goal of the reform process was to design a program that all parties could support, the group faced strong pressure to find a compromise that had broad appeal. The nonsocialist parties also were anxious to avoid an argument over pension reform that could threaten the stability of the government.

The mission was to design a fiscally sustainable system tied to economic growth and with a clear link between contributions and benefits. To achieve this, the following principles guided the reform discussions: benefits should be determined by contributions from lifetime earnings, indexation should be based on the growth of the contribution base, and benefits at retirement should incorporate changes in life expectancy.[7] It was equally important that the contribution rate should remain unchanged in the future. Total payroll taxes are high in Sweden, and the common view was that it was not possible to introduce a system in which the contribution rate would drift upward. Because of the desire to create a close link between contributions and benefits while holding contribution rates steady, the group favored the introduction of a defined contribution plan but within a primarily pay-as-you-go system. The group also agreed that some of the large public buffer funds should be moved into the private financial markets. The result was the NDC plan, with a funded component that includes individual accounts.[8]

HOW DOES THE REFORMED SWEDISH PENSION SYSTEM WORK?

In the reformed public pension system, earnings-related benefits come from two components: the NDC pay-as-you-go plan and the Premium Pension plan of funded individual accounts. The overall contribution rate is 18.5 percent of earnings up to a ceiling; 16 percent is credited toward the NDC, and 2.5 percent is channeled to the

Premium Pension. Contributions are split equally between employees and employers. Employees' contributions are limited by a ceiling, while the employer's share is levied on all earnings. Individuals also earn credits for child care years and time in military service and in education, as well as for sickness insurance benefits and unemployment insurance.

For individuals with no or low earnings-related benefits, the system provides a guaranteed pension to ensure a minimum standard of living in retirement. The guaranteed benefit is means-tested and offset by whatever income is generated through the NDC component. It is financed by general tax revenues and is in that way separated from the earnings-related system.[9] The guaranteed pension is the main tool for redistribution in the new system. The benefit is quite generous; approximately 40 percent of retirees will collect at least some pension income via this safeguard.[10]

THE NDC COMPONENT

The main part of the reformed pension system is the NDC. The essential idea of a pay-as-you-go system based on defined contributions is the same as in a conventional defined contribution system. Contributions are recorded in individual accounts, and the account values represent individuals' claims on future pension benefits. But, unlike in a conventional defined contribution system, annual contributions are used to finance current pension benefit obligations as in any pay-as-you-go system.[11] Hence, the individual accounts are notional.

The account balance grows with annual contributions and the rate of return on the account. In order to link earned pension rights to the income of the active population, the rate of return is set to equal the per capita wage growth. Alternatively, the rate of return could have been determined by total wage growth. However, an important goal of the reform was to ensure that earned pension rights and benefits followed the growth in average wages for the active population and that individuals' earnings had the same effect on their pension incomes whenever they were earned in the course of their lifetime. It was deemed that this would best be achieved by using per capita wage growth.

TABLE 5.3. INDEXATION OF PENSION BENEFITS AFTER RETIREMENT

| | Wage Growth | | |
	Equal to Norm	Less than Norm	Greater than Norm
Real wage growth	1.6%	0.5%	2.5%
Deviation from 1.6% growth norm	0.0	-1.1	0.9
Inflation	2.0%	2.0%	2.0%
Pension benefits changed by:	2.0%	0.9%	2.9%

Source: Author's calculations.

Retirement age is flexible, and benefits can be withdrawn from age sixty-one onward. At retirement, initial annual benefits are calculated by dividing the balance in the notional account by an annuity divisor. The divisor is determined by average life expectancy at retirement for men and women together for a given cohort at age sixty-five and an imputed annual real rate of return of 1.6 percent. Thus, the divisor is the same for men and women. Since the annual pension benefit is equal to the net present value of future benefits using a real interest rate of 1.6, the initial benefit at retirement is higher than if benefits based on the current value of the account were adjusted for economic growth each year. The reasoning behind providing a substantial initial benefit rather than having an increasing benefit profile was to meet the relatively higher consumption needs at the beginning of the retirement period. The divisor is fixed at retirement and will not be adjusted for later changes in life expectancy for a given cohort.

Benefits are then indexed annually to consumer prices. The fact that the initial benefit includes an implicit real rate of return means that retirees have received an advance tied to projected 1.6 percent real long-term growth. What happens if long-term growth falls short of 1.6 percent? To maintain financial stability and to avoid overcompensating retirees relative to the working population, the price indexing of benefits is adjusted to reflect the deviation from this growth norm. Table 5.3 provides an example of the indexation of postretirement benefits.

If real wage growth in the economy is equal to 1.6 percent, pension benefits will be adjusted by the full price increase (Table 5.3, column 1). However, if growth falls below the norm, pensioners will not be compensated fully for price increases (column 2). Over a worker's lifetime this type of indexation gives the same result as straightforward wage indexation.[12]

THE INDIVIDUAL ACCOUNT: THE PREMIUM PENSION

One of the main objectives of funded individual accounts was to help increase saving in Sweden.[13] The individual account component is a "carve-out": of the 18.5 percent total contribution rate, 2.5 percentage points go to the individual accounts.[14] A new government agency, the Premium Pension Agency (Premiepensionsmyndigheten, or PPM), has been established to administer the funded accounts and will serve as a clearinghouse. The PPM also acts as the sole provider of annuities in the funded system. The accounts are self-directed; participants can choose among several hundred domestic and international funds and are allowed to invest in up to five funds.[15] Any fund that is licensed to do business in Sweden is allowed to participate in the system, and since inception the number of funds has increased from about 450 to about 600.[16] For individuals who do not make a choice, a default fund managed by the government has been set up. The default option is mainly invested in global equities (currently the fund holds 65 percent in international equities and 17 percent in Swedish equities). Contributions are invested by the PPM in lump sums; hence the fund companies will know only the total investment of pension contributions, not who the individual investors are. The first investments in the Premium Pension took place in 2000, and roughly two-thirds of participants made an investment decision; the assets for the remaining one-third were invested in the default fund. Among those who decided how to allocate their funds, almost 75 percent invested in equity funds and on average chose 3.4 funds.

At retirement, any time after age sixty-one, the account balance will be converted to a mandatory fixed or variable annuity. The introduction of an individual account component means that part of the pension benefit will depend on participants' investment behavior.[17] Because portfolios will have different returns, a consequence might be that pension benefits will be more unequally distributed.

THE TRANSITION

The transition to the new system will be implemented over sixteen years.[18] The first to participate in the system are those born in 1938; they will receive one-fifth of their benefit from the new system and four-fifths from the old system. Each annual cohort will then increase its participation in the new system by five percentage points, so that those born in 1944 will receive half of their benefit from the reformed system and half from the old system. Those born in 1954 or later will participate only in the new system.[19]

Benefits will not be paid completely from the new system until 2040. This means that in 2015, soon after the baby-boom generation has begun to retire, even though new retirees will get most of their benefits under the reformed system, a large share of total benefits will still be paid from the old system. Financial pressures will remain in the pension system because of the large relative size of the baby-boom generation.

FINANCIAL STABILITY

One of the critical challenges of the pension reform was to design a system that would be financially stable over time, even when faced with adverse demographic and economic developments. However, since the system is still pay-as-you-go, the government has to cover its pension liability through annual contributions. Increasing the contribution rate is not a workable option in the NDC framework since it automatically increases benefit promises. Therefore, the buffer funds and the introduction of an automatic balancing mechanism are essential for financial stability.

THE BUFFER FUNDS

The buffer funds play an important role in the implementation of the new pension system. In the short term, the funds will alleviate the pressures on the general budget brought to bear by the reform. Some programs—the disability pension and survivor pension—that previously were financed through payroll taxes will now be financed through general tax revenues. In order to offset this burden, about one-third of the balance in the buffer funds was transferred in 1999, 2000, and 2001 to the general budget.[20]

In the long run, the buffer funds are needed to cover projected deficits in the financing of benefits when the large baby-boom generation starts to retire. Although the pension reform creates a system that is fiscally stable in the long run, it cannot by itself accommodate the retirement of the baby-boom cohorts.

Given the importance of the buffer funds for supporting the new pension scheme, the governance and investment rules of the funds have been reevaluated. In the past, the buffer funds have been criticized for sacrificing returns in order to achieve political goals, in particular the subsidization of housing. The new investment rules require that investments be made on risk and return considerations only. The guidelines also allow a larger share to be invested in equities and international assets.

AUTOMATIC BALANCING

Because the system remains pay-as-you-go, it is still sensitive to demographic change. Two particular features in the design of the system could introduce financial instability. The first is the indexation of benefits to average wage growth rather than to the growth in total wages. The second is the use of fixed divisors in the NDC annuity calculations.

Earned pension rights and current benefits are indexed to follow the growth in the per capita wage, while contributions are determined by the growth in total wages. A decline in the size of the workforce means that average wages outpace total wages, so that benefit claims grow faster than the contributions that are financing them. While the growth of total wages might have been used for indexing instead, as noted above, the reform aimed to ensure that earned pension rights followed the growth in average wages for the active population and that individuals' benefits were not affected by when they were earned.

The retirement annuity is based on the current longevity of a cohort when it reaches age sixty-five rather than on a projection of that cohort's life expectancy. The divisors are fixed and not adjusted to take into account changes in life span. If it turns out that actual longevity for a given cohort is greater than that used to calculate the divisor, their total benefit payments will exceed their total contributions.

In order to deal with these two sources of financial instability, an automatic balancing mechanism has been introduced. When automatic balancing is applied to deal with a deficit, per capita wage indexation is reduced to bring the system back into balance. As indicated by its name, the mechanism does not require any action by politicians. Those who devised the pension reform felt it was important that the system be shielded from discretionary changes and that the risk of manipulation for political gain be minimized. An autonomous system was deemed necessary to maintain credibility and for the system to survive in the long run.

The introduction of automatic balancing requires that a measure of financial stability be calculated. Prior to the reform, the National Social Insurance Board undertook traditional projections in order to set the contribution rate. The new pension system included provisions for the kind of information about financial status needed, to be made public in an annual report that includes an income statement as well as a balance sheet. A balance ratio that relates the pension system's assets to its liabilities also is calculated annually. The balance ratio is defined as follows:

Balance ratio = (Capitalized Value of Contributions + Buffer Funds) / Pension Liability

The assets consist of the capitalized value of contributions and the current value of the buffer funds. The capitalized value of contributions is derived by multiplying annual contributions by the turnover duration. The turnover duration is the expected average time between when a contribution is made to the system and when the benefit payment based on that contribution is made. (The inverse of the turnover duration is the discount rate of the flow of contributions.) The current turnover duration is approximately thirty-two years.[21] On the opposite side of the ledger is the current vested liability for pension claims.[22] A balance ratio of one, with assets equal to liabilities, means that the NDC system is in financial balance. If the balance ratio is below one, liabilities exceed assets and the system is in imbalance; if the balance ratio exceeds one, the system has an accumulated surplus. Table 5.4 (see page 78) shows the financial balance of the NDC in 2001 and 2002.

TABLE 5.4. ASSETS AND LIABILITIES, NOTIONAL DEFINED
CONTRIBUTION, 2001 AND 2002 (MILLIONS OF SWEDISH CROWNS)

	2001	2002	Change	Percentage Change
Contribution assets	5,085,252	5,292,764	207,512	-13.7
Buffer funds	56,171	487,539	-77,632	4.1
Total assets	5,650,423	5,780,303	129,880	2.3
Pension liability	5,423,016	5,728,658	296,642	5.5
Assets minus liabilities	218,407	51,645	-166,762	-76.4
Balance ratio	1.04	1.01	-0.03	-2.9

Note: At the time of this study, one U.S. dollar was equal to approximately seven Swedish crowns.

Source: Swedish Pension System, Annual Report 2002.

The automatic balance mechanism is activated as soon as the balance ratio falls below one, at which point the indexation of earned pension rights and current benefits is reduced below average wage growth. The reduction is calculated by multiplying the change in average wage growth by the balance ratio. (To smooth out the effects of temporary downturns, a three-year moving average is used in the calculation of the balance ratio.) The reduced indexation will continue as long as the balance ratio is less than one.

Currently the automatic balancing mechanism is applied only in the event of a deficit. However, it is possible that the system would build up a permanent (and substantial) surplus under certain economic and demographic conditions. The policymakers in the pension group have agreed that if the surplus becomes "larger than what is motivated," the excess should be distributed to the participants. The question is, naturally, what is meant by "larger than what is motivated." A government inquiry is now analyzing the issue. Its task is to determine the balance ratio at which a distribution could be made without threatening the system's financial stability. Of course, it is not likely that a surplus distribution will occur anytime soon. However, the issue is being worked through now so as to maintain an autonomous system—future governments should not be tempted to use the buffer funds for purposes other than to pay pension benefits.

IMPLICATIONS OF THE AUTOMATIC ADJUSTMENTS

The benefits of a financially stable system as well as the advantages of a system where all adjustments are made automatically are clear. But what are the implications of the Swedish design for individuals' retirement income and the distribution of income within and between generations?

Because the contribution rate in an NDC is fixed by definition, all adjustments to ensure the system's financial stability are made on the benefit side. This means that the system shifts the risk of financing benefits from future generations to the current one.

The activation of the automatic balancing mechanism reduces the indexation of earned pension rights and current benefits by the same amount. This has implications for the distribution of benefits between cohorts since a person in the beginning of his or her career has a longer horizon to recoup the loss in benefits than does a retiree who has started to collect benefits.

The calculation of benefits is indexed to life expectancy through the annuity divisor. When average life expectancy increases, individuals will have to work longer to reach a given replacement rate (replacing a percentage of prior earnings). For some groups, such as those with physically demanding jobs, this may be difficult, and they may end up with lower replacement rates than in a system that adjusted both contributions and benefits.

CONCLUSION

The Swedish public pension reform took almost a decade. The new system generally puts more responsibility on the individual to plan and prepare for retirement. The benefits in the NDC are determined by lifetime contributions, and the system also includes a funded individual account. However, the focus on contributions makes benefits less transparent. In the old defined benefit system, the benefit formula clearly indicated the replacement rate, and it was relatively easy for workers to estimate expected benefits at retirement. Because benefits in the new system are not defined but depend on contributions, it is difficult to express the expected benefit in terms of a replacement rate. It is difficult as well to estimate future benefits because they vary with the rate of return and life expectancy. An additional complexity stems from the way benefits are indexed after retirement. A major challenge in the coming years will be to provide information and education to help participants make sound decisions about retirement, savings, and work.

The Swedish experience with pension reform provides some important lessons for other countries considering reform. In particular, the Swedish policymakers recognized that pension systems are dynamic institutions and must adjust to changing demographic and economic circumstances. They also recognized that it may be politically difficult to make the necessary adjustments. They therefore "tied their hands" by introducing a set of automatic stabilizers. If the system comes under financial pressure, this automatic adjustment could lead to benefit cuts. Because the Swedish system provides a minimum guaranteed benefit that is well above the poverty level, responding to hard times only through trimming benefits may be less of a problem than in countries with lower benefit floors. For such countries, pension schemes in which adjustment takes place both on the benefit and the contribution side may be preferable.

The introduction of funded individual accounts was one area of much disagreement in the reform process. In the end, a small funded pillar with very broad investment choice was introduced. However, the investment experiences during the first three years underscore the importance of a well-designed default fund. Another topic of interest to countries considering the introduction of individual accounts is whether the clearinghouse model will be cost-effective in the long run. Plan administration of the Swedish individual account component requires a well-developed infrastructure, and plan implementation has been more costly and complicated than anticipated.

6.

PERSPECTIVES ON INDIVIDUAL RESPONSIBILITY AND SOCIAL INSURANCE

Van Doorn Ooms, Maya C. MacGuineas, Jerry L. Mashaw,
William A. Niskanen, and John H. Langbein

This chapter contains four papers that examine several larger and broader issues, including those that concern values that often lie hidden behind discussions of social insurance. These issues can be framed under a rubric of "individual versus collective responsibility." This categorization, of course, is by no means comprehensive, and the papers look into a number of interesting issues that fall outside the framework.

THE PAPERS

Maya C. MacGuineas's paper, "Paying for Retirement," raises several big-picture questions about financing Social Security and Medicare: What share of national resources should be committed to these programs? Who bears the risks, and who ultimately pays? What public or private mechanisms would best serve our purposes? In "Social Insurance and the American Social Contract," Jerry L. Mashaw examines the values inherent in the social contract and asks how they relate to the goals and techniques of social insurance, urging us to focus on the underlying values of personal and family responsibility and fairness rather than on particular financing mechanisms. William A. Niskanen's provocative paper, "Increasing Individual Responsibility Would Increase Retirement Security," calls for a radical policy shift away from the current tax-financed structures of Social Security and Medicare, which he views as unsustainable and, for that reason and others, ultimately ineffective. Niskanen advocates allowing workers the option of diverting their share of the payroll tax to individual, private accounts. Finally, John H. Langbein's "Social Security and the Private Pension System" contrasts the rationale, structure, and impact of Social Security with those of our private (but heavily tax-subsidized) pension system, finding that they effectively serve very different purposes and benefit different income groups in the society.

WHAT IS SOCIAL INSURANCE?

These papers, like many discussions of the subject, convey divergent views of the meaning of the term "social insurance," either explicitly or implicitly. MacGuineas raises the issue directly, noting the difference between insuring against poverty or catastrophic health care costs in old age and providing universal benefits that are relatively independent of need or circumstance. Mashaw agrees that first-dollar, comprehensive coverage is not necessarily the objective of health care insurance, which may appropriately incorporate copayments and deductibles and pay for some services out-of-pocket.

There is a tension between the "insurance" and "benefits" concepts that fuels important differences between the various authors presented here regarding the goals of social insurance programs. Mashaw believes that the goal of social insurance should be "reasonable income security" over the life cycle, that "basic guarantees should not fall below current levels," and that such programs have an important redistributive function—a view that Langbein supports. Niskanen, by contrast, would preserve a public safety net at 120 percent of the poverty threshold in Social Security while "carving out" half of the payroll tax for capital accumulation in personal accounts. Mashaw's emphasis on the provision necessary for income security undoubtedly accords more closely with the conventional public understanding of "social insurance," while Niskanen's looks more like genuine insurance. It is important to note, however, that, despite these major differences, all the authors appear to accept the importance of universal coverage for maximizing the risk pool in Social Security and Medicare.

The distinction between insurance and entitlement benefits has grown more important in recent years as Social Security benefits more frequently have become supplementary incomes during second careers and the pressures to expand Medicare coverage have increased. Conflict between the two likely will sharpen as the country enters an era of fiscal austerity upon the retirement of the baby boomers beginning at the end of this decade. Universal coverage and relatively liberal benefits will command strong political support and will at the same time make unprecedented peacetime demands on public resources. As MacGuineas notes, Social Security and Medicare are projected to consume nearly 15 percent of GDP by 2050, about twice their current share. As significant benefit cuts or tax increases eventually become imperative, American politics will be severely challenged. Niskanen, in fact, sees "no politically feasible way" to maintain health care and retirement security through tax financing.

DIMENSIONS OF THE SOCIAL CONTRACT

What underlies the "social contract," to which such easy appeal is made in discussions of social insurance programs? In examining this question, it may be useful to distinguish the social contract between generations from that within generations.

The intergenerational contract. As Langbein notes, Social Security to a large degree has replaced a traditional system of support for the elderly that was based on family, or small community, ties. The evolving public system effectively socialized and institutionalized the support of retired workers (and, more often, their widows) that had been supplied by their children or other close relations. The "contract" is that "I will support everyone's parents while I work and will expect everyone's kids to support me when I retire." A collective, universal, mandatory system spreads the risk of destitution broadly over the society at large, yielding substantial economic and social benefits.

This change has both derived from and reinforced a highly mobile population and labor force in a large and rapidly changing society and economy.

The broad socialization of risk, however, as with any insurance arrangement, inevitably introduces an element of what economists call "moral hazard" that, to some degree, weakens individual responsibility. If I am reasonably confident of coming into a substantial family inheritance, I am likely to consume more and save less of my income; it is hardly surprising that Social Security and Medicare would dampen the enthusiasm for retirement saving and extended working lives.

The degree of socialization of risk in a social insurance system has clear implications for its financing. A stronger emphasis on individual, as opposed to collective, responsibility implies more "prefunding" of benefits (whereby an individual accumulates assets over his lifetime to pay for retirement) and less "pay-as-you-go" resource transfer from current workers to current retirees. Thus, Niskanen, strongly supporting personal responsibility, would push social insurance sharply toward prefunding, with private accounts for Social Security and defined contributions for Medicare. MacGuineas, less emphatically, also foresees a greater role for individual accounts in preparing for retirement. Even Mashaw, who strongly supports the general structure of the current system, notes that retirement security might be enhanced if Social Security portfolios included claims on capital assets as well as on the incomes of current workers.

The intergenerational "contract" is commonly discussed simply in terms of direct income transfers into and out of some funding mechanism, such as the Social Security or Medicare trust funds. However, indirect intergenerational transfers of wealth through changes in national saving, investment, and economic growth also are important when considering programs as large as Social Security and Medicare. The conventional wisdom, expressed by MacGuineas in her plea for recognition of the need for national saving, is that future workers will be burdened by heavy costs of supporting retired baby boomers. We therefore should transfer resources to the future by consuming less and saving more now, principally by reducing current budget deficits. However, the degree to which this should be done is unclear, especially if the means of reducing current consumption is unspecified. Those next generations, after all, will probably be wealthier than the current generation (in spite of their demographic burden) and certainly wealthier, on average, than low-income members of this generation. Thus, the specific content of deficit reduction policies to increase growth is critically important in striving to improve equity.

The Intragenerational Contract

Most Americans understand the social contract to involve relationships within as well as across generations. What obligations do we owe to others in our society outside the circle of family and those with whom we have close personal relations? Individualism and the rewards to personal endeavor appear to run stronger in our diverse society and market-oriented economy than in most other industrialized nations. But, as Mashaw notes, economic rewards are not created by individual endeavor alone. Economic success also depends upon laws and institutions that protect property, economic relationships that promote cooperation and trust, the fit between one's personal capacities and the public's demand for goods and services, and often simply luck, especially with regard to the circumstances of birth and early development.

For this reason, the viability of a capitalist economy that yields substantial inequality as a by-product requires a set of rules that are accepted as fair and confer legitimacy on the system. Mashaw emphasizes the principles of equal opportunity, "just deserts," social responsibility for risks beyond individual control, and progressive financing of arrangements to implement these principles. Of course, this involves redistribution of economic resources. What costs are entailed by such redistribution, and how extensive should it be? Two issues involved here are liberty and incentives for work and saving.

Langbein reminds us that Social Security is paternalistic and compulsory; the benefits of universality are secured at the cost of interference with individual liberty. Assessment of this trade-off is a "bright line" separating views on how extensive redistributive arrangements should be. Mashaw refers to a "vast agenda of social insurance reform that invites our attention." In sharp distinction, Niskanen would significantly curtail the redistributive effects of Social Security (and probably Medicare) in order to secure more individual choice through private retirement accounts and individually defined health insurance contributions.

A second issue pertaining to the intragenerational social contract is the effect of economic transfers on work effort and saving. The magnitude of such effects on incentives is controversial. These papers do not address the issue explicitly, although the goal of enhancing incentives is implicit in Niskanen's discussion. Whether public goals, such as retirement security, are well served by policies that purport to pursue them by providing economic incentives depends critically upon their design. Langbein pointedly notes that "the so-called private pension system is only incidentally about retirement income" and that the tax subsidies that support defined contribution plans have instead created "multipurpose savings, investment, and wealth transmission vehicles for the tax-sensitive classes."

Work and saving incentives have been of more interest to policy analysts than to the public and have not yet become politically salient in considerations of Social Security and Medicare. One should note, however, the major role they came to play in public discussions of the welfare reform legislation of 1996. As the pressure to modify social insurance programs increases in anticipation of the fiscal difficulties that lie ahead, questions about the incentive effect of such programs and any proposed modifications on individual behavior are likely to be raised. This will inevitably invite a more wide-ranging public discussion of the appropriate balance between personal and collective responsibility in social insurance.

PAYING FOR RETIREMENT

Maya C. MacGuineas

INTRODUCTION

True or false? The federal government is little more than an ATM for seniors that manages the armed forces on the side. How one responds to this quip is a pretty good indication of how one views the growing costs of retirement in the United States. There are those who nod their heads in agreement (a group that generally believes in the need to implement significant structural reforms) and those who roll their eyes at the exaggeration (a group more content to make incremental changes and wait until it becomes absolutely necessary to do so).

The issue, however, is broader than just the share of government resources dedicated to retirement costs, which can include everything from Social Security and pension benefits to health insurance and direct health care costs to tax revenues forgone for the sake of encouraging individual saving for retirement needs. Thus, a comprehensive look at the question of how this country will pay for retirement costs in the future must examine the share of the entire economy that is dedicated to the nonworking elderly and the extent to which we defer consumption today in order to allow ourselves to consume more tomorrow.

In taking such a comprehensive view of paying for retirement, there are four questions that must be considered. What share of national resources should be dedicated to retirement costs? How should the burden of paying for retirement costs be distributed? Who should shoulder the risk? What structures should be used?

WHAT SHARE OF RESOURCES?

If the federal government's two major retirement programs, Social Security and Medicare, continue to grow on their current projected paths, they will consume a share of GDP that will more than double to nearly 15 percent by 2050. Significant growth in the cost of government employee and veterans' pensions will add to the budgeting dilemma legislators will soon face. Since the nation cannot run larger and larger deficits forever, these circumstances leave only three alternatives:

1. Raise taxes to cover all the promised benefits and allow federal expenditures to grow to an unprecedented size;

2. Reduce other areas of government spending to make room for higher retirement costs, thereby squeezing out priorities such as public investment, defense, and other safety net programs;

3. Slow the growth of promised retirement benefits.

While there are legitimate arguments in favor of each of these approaches, a continued emphasis on consumption-based transfer programs at the expense of public investment is likely to impair future economic growth and will diminish budgetary flexibility. Certainly, the past several years have demonstrated that there is no way confidently to anticipate all future budgetary needs, whether in providing national security, protecting the environment, or helping to smooth out rocky transitions in an increasingly global marketplace. Allowing ample room to cover unexpected costs is a necessary practice for prudent budgeting.

Just as the public sector faces the resource demands of an aging population, so too will the private sector. Though the trend of companies shifting from defined benefit to defined contribution plans is well under way, defined benefit plans remain an important part of the pensions landscape. As of the end of 2003, such plans were underfunded by roughly $400 billion. Making good on these retirement promises will shift company resources away from productive expenditures such as compensation and investment. This is likely to depress businesses' bottom line and economic performance. As market barriers continue to fall and global competition increases, these additional costs will leave U.S. businesses at a competitive disadvantage.

Who Pays?

There are only three sources of financing to cover the major retirement expenditures: governments (ultimately, taxpayers), businesses (ultimately, their shareholders, workers, or customers), and individuals. Each may be suited to different goals. If the objective of retirement policy is to compel individuals to prepare for old age, government mandates may be needed. By removing the elements of choice that exist in individual saving or voluntary, employer-based pension schemes, universal coverage of target populations is ensured. Public/private hybrid approaches, where the government uses tax incentives to encourage individuals to prepare for their own retirement, are likely to be less successful and more expensive since those who take advantage of the incentives would often have participated without them. More important, those who would not participate without incentives may still fail to do so.

Likewise, a centralized provider such as the government is best equipped to counteract typical insurance market failures such as cases of adverse selection. Thus, if policymakers determined, for example, that some kind of catastrophic health insurance policy should be required for the entire population, the government would be instrumental in creating a risk-pooling mechanism.

Finally, if retirement security involves redistribution, such as transfers to the poor or from workers to stay-at-home parents, government involvement is necessary.

Businesses can play several useful roles. They can serve as centralized administrators; 401(k) programs, for example, have benefited greatly from the automatic deduction options provided by employers, and take-up rates are much higher than they would be if businesses were not involved. Another major contribution businesses can provide is risk pooling for health insurance, allowing both workers and retirees to participate in private plans they could not otherwise afford on their own.

Obviously, there is a role for individuals in preparing for their own retirement so that they are able to replace lost employment income and to help cover their health care costs, whether for insurance premiums, copayments, or direct medical costs.

In the end, individuals pay for retirement costs no matter what pass-through, centralizing, or administrative mechanisms are used to provide them. In the case of the government as provider, individuals bear the costs through taxes. In the case of employer-provided benefits, the cost comes back to individuals in the form of lower wages to workers, higher prices to consumers, or lower returns to investors. So not only are different mechanisms more or less appropriate depending on the policy objectives, but each has major implications for just which individuals will bear the cost.

Who Bears the Risk?

Related to the issue of who pays for retirement is that of who bears the associated risks. In the past, retirees were insulated from many risks. In its earlier decades, Social Security benefits were often liberalized (even if irregularly) to be larger than promised, not smaller, and most private pensions were defined benefit plans. Furthermore, the government stepped up to cover a far greater share of Medicare

(Part B) than was originally intended. These arrangements left the government (meaning taxpayers) rather than benefit recipients, employees, and investors shouldering the risk of higher than anticipated retirement costs.

More recently, trends have moved in a different direction. Significant Social Security benefit reductions were signed into law in the 1983 reforms, and more cutbacks are likely in the future to help contain the program's costs and close its projected deficits. (As the debate continues about whether to include integrated individual accounts as part of a modernized Social Security system, risk is one of the major issues dividing people into opposing camps. Those who object to private accounts cite the investment risk that retirees would face if their individual account portfolios underperformed. But the political risk that benefits promised under the current system will be cut is an equally important consideration.)

Furthermore, it will no longer be as easy or as fair to insulate senior citizens from the risks they face in retirement as they become an ever-larger segment of the population. It makes little sense to ask workers to shoulder the risks of employer-based and government-provided benefits while sheltering retirees, particularly when many workers are less well off than retirees. A fairer approach would be to diversify the risks involved and to spread them more equitably across the entire population while taking into consideration an individual's ability to shoulder certain risks.

What Structure?

There are a number of approaches to crafting retirement policies. The first approach involves direct outlays by either the public or private sector. The government can spend on its own programs, or businesses can include defined benefit pension plans as part of their compensation packages. Since defined benefit plans are generally reinsured by the government, taxpayers still face liabilities.

An alternative approach is to use incentives to change private behavior. The government employs a number of tax incentives to encourage individuals to save on their own behalf, including the deductibility of many types of retirement saving. Likewise, employer-provided matches for 401(k) accounts provide private incentives. Finally, mandates or regulations can be used to structure retirement policy. For instance, there is a growing interest in mandating individual insurance for those without other health coverage. A number of Democratic presidential candidates in 2004 proposed insurance mandates to cover children. Employee Retirement Income Security Act (ERISA) laws are another example of requirements that are used to expand coverage and participation.

POTENTIAL STRUCTURAL CHANGES

Beyond the basic issues, there are a number of larger, conceptual questions that need to be answered. These surround the need to increase saving, the distinction between social insurance and social benefits, the role of employers in providing benefits, and the need to control health care costs.

THE NEED FOR SAVING

Higher levels of saving and investment are essential to reduce the burden of paying for future retirement benefits by raising economic growth. For that reason, low personal saving rates, which are now compounded by the return of structural government budget deficits, are particularly troubling in that they hurt both individuals' retirement prospects and the economy at large. Our heavy reliance on foreign capital to replace this deficiency of saving has not to date proved to be overly burdensome for the economy. However, declines in the dollar and other countries' eventual need for their saving to contend with their own demographic challenges imply that continued reliance on foreign capital could leave the U.S. economy in a severely vulnerable and weakened position. Therefore, policies that would enhance personal and national saving would have the dual benefits of setting aside resources today to pay for individual well-being in the future while strengthening the overall economy.

Many economists believe that the structure of Social Security, which promises workers who live to retirement age a steady, inflation-adjusted retirement benefit, reduces personal saving rates because workers feel less urgency to save on their own. Likewise, the presence of the Medicare program reduces the imperative for individuals to save for future costs of their own medical care. Thus, it is not surprising that the expansion of insurance and government benefits for health and pension needs has been correlated with lower levels of personal saving.

If consensus is reached that the way in which retirement benefits are paid for and delivered should be consistent with the objective of increasing national saving, this will necessitate shifting toward policies that either increase government saving, require businesses to set aside resources with which to pay promised benefits, or encourage (or compel) individuals to save in order to cover more of their own retirement expenses. Any such policies will need to be structured to create net increases in national saving rather than just higher personal saving that is offset by saving incentives that enlarge the budget deficit.

SOCIAL INSURANCE OR SOCIAL BENEFITS?

The United States will have to grapple with the question, "What is the true meaning of social insurance?" Our largest government programs, Social Security and Medicare, treat social insurance and universal benefits as one and the same. However, there is a difference between insuring retirees against poverty or catastrophic health care costs in old age and providing universal benefits regardless of need or circumstance. The latter, which describes our current social contract, leads to the all too common situation of low-income workers supporting more affluent retirees. These programs are universal in part to guarantee ongoing political support. However, their immense cost will certainly become more difficult to accommodate as budgetary pressures increase.

An alternative structure would focus more on the insurance aspects of the social contract. Retirees who had contributed over their working lifetimes would be protected against living in poverty and catastrophic health care costs. Beyond that, retirees of small means could be subsidized further either through government matches to their saving during their working years or through provision of additional benefits during retirement. Significant savings would be realized from shifting the qualifications for government transfer programs from age to need, moving away from a system of universal benefits to one of true social insurance.

The Role of Employers

Employers are now viewed as an integral part of the social contract, but this arrangement was an accident of history dating back to wage and price rationing during World War II. The resulting reliance on employers to play a central role in providing both health and retirement benefits has both positive and negative effects. On the one hand, employers provide the useful services of automatic withdrawals for retirement saving and risk pooling for health insurance. On the other hand, linking retirement benefits to jobs can hinder job mobility. Moreover, it perpetuates the misconception that the responsibility for preparing for retirement can and should be borne by employers (and, by extension, the government) when in reality the costs are shifted back to individuals through a variety of less transparent channels.

Furthermore, the tax-based incentives that encourage employers to provide such benefits are highly regressive and often ineffective. Exempting employer-provided health care and retirement benefits from income tax provides the largest tax breaks for those who need them least. Furthermore, these tax preferences, which are the largest tax expenditures, contribute to the complexity and inefficiencies in the income tax code. Finally, if policymakers continue to shift our hybrid tax system from an emphasis on income tax to a consumption tax basis, it will become increasingly difficult to use the tax code to create targeted saving incentives for particular groups of people or purposes.

Containing Health Care Costs

It will be necessary to figure out ways to contain spiraling health care costs, which currently are the most powerful driver of the projections of unsustainable federal expenditures. While health care rationing is not yet a serious topic of national discussion, it is likely to emerge in coming years.

Apart from that, however, a structural reworking of health insurance—of both the incentives built into the system and the procedures covered—could make a significant difference. Currently, health care consumers are far too divorced from the actual costs of the services they receive. Prices are not transparent, so even a consumer who is attempting to be price conscious has a difficult time doing so. The subsidies and favorable tax treatment of health insurance and health care provision lead to overconsumption and higher costs. This is exacerbated because so many minor health care services are covered by insurance. In general, one does not insure a house for gutter cleanings but does so for fire damage. One insures a car for collisions but not for oil changes. Yet, health insurance coverage normally covers such routine procedures as dental cleanings, eye exams, and checkups. At the same time, certain major health care costs are capped in terms of reimbursement, undermining the basic purpose of insurance as a protection against large financial risk. Thus, a fundamental reworking of the health insurance market that relinked consumers to ongoing, predictable expenditures while protecting them against unanticipated and severe contingencies would help contain spiraling health care costs.

Conclusion

Whether or not the preceding suggestions for major structural changes in how retirement benefits are provided get implemented, certain trends away from the current arrangements seem inexorable. First, the nation will adopt more flexible retirement ages. The retirement crisis the country will face also will present a labor market problem as the pool of labor resources stagnates and economic growth slows. Finding ways to encourage individuals to spend more years in the workforce will be critical in containing retirement costs and ensuring that the elderly are sufficiently provided for once they do stop working. The notion that a set retirement age best meets the individual needs of hundreds of millions of workers is clearly wrong. Many who become disabled will need to retire earlier than the current normal retirement age, while many others will find that they are both eager and able to stay in the workforce longer.

Second, individual accounts will play a greater role in preparing for retirement. Whether these accounts are used to augment or replace existing government and employer-based programs, it seems certain that they will become a more integral part of the social contract. Accordingly, public and private policies will respond to the more widespread use of such individual accounts. Low levels of financial literacy in the country will have to be overcome. Furthermore, given the significant share of the population without bank accounts, both public and private sector efforts are likely to emerge to link citizens to financial institutions. In addition, the annuities market, which remains relatively underdeveloped in the United States, should grow significantly. Beyond providing a mechanism to ensure that individuals do not dissipate or outlive their savings, annuities send important signals about adequate saving levels. For instance, by comparing personal savings with annuity prices, a fifty-five-year-old can see whether he or she is on track to retire with a monthly income that will meet (or surpass) anticipated needs or whether the best course of action is to start saving more or to plan on working longer than originally expected.

Finally, one of the problems with some of the nation's saving instruments—particularly with regard to housing and 401(k)s—has been the increasing popularity of borrowing against one's savings. Since leaving the workforce with an individual saving account and a corresponding liability will do little good in terms of covering retirement costs, it is likely that new regulations prohibiting or at least discouraging borrowing against many of these tax-favored or mandated savings vehicles will have to be implemented.

SOCIAL INSURANCE AND THE AMERICAN SOCIAL CONTRACT

Jerry L. Mashaw

Talk about social insurance and social insurance reform in the United States has been going on for more than one hundred years. The intensity of the debate waxes and wanes, tending to wax particularly in presidential election years. Yet, reformers of various stripes, proponents of diverse plans and defenders of the status quo, often have much more in common than the tenor of the debate suggests. For there is substantial agreement among Americans about the values that are represented by the American social contract and about the goals of social insurance in implementing and securing some of those values. The disagreements are often more about techniques and mechanisms.

Techniques and mechanisms are hardly unimportant. The success or workability of any particular program is often highly dependent upon its details, and some debates about techniques are really about values and goals. But techniques and mechanisms do not define what social insurance is, can be, or should be. Instead, values and goals should be placed at the forefront of the conversation, and instruments to further those ideals should be evaluated accordingly, not in terms of whether they advance some cherished model of social insurance.

THE VALUES EMBEDDED IN THE AMERICAN SOCIAL CONTRACT

Americans live in what is often described as a mixed economy: an economy based on freedom of contract and market competition, combined with collective action that both regulates the market and modifies its outcomes. The values that guide this mixed economy are the twin pillars of personal or family responsibility and what can best be called "shared luck."

This country firmly believes in the primacy of personal and family responsibility for individual well-being. We all recognize responsibilities that are broader than ourselves and our families, but, when push comes to shove, these duties are satisfied only after we satisfy our obligations to ourselves and to our closest kin. We believe that everyone (or at least every healthy adult) is responsible for his or her own economic well-being and for that of close family and dependents. Families are expected to be "self-supporting" for the most part.

But this notion that people are responsible for their own economic circumstances carries only so far. Everyone operates in an economic system that binds its participants together through particular rules for promoting economic cooperation, settling conflicts, and allocating resources. Horatio Alger stories of personal triumph aside, individual success also is a function of the success of the economy as a whole and of the organization of its market, legal, and social systems. Our capacity to support ourselves depends critically on others' willingness to engage with us in a complex system of productive activity.

In any such system of market capitalism there is typically a considerable dispersion in individual returns to economic participation.

Those returns depend on the public's demand for particular services and goods. People who work or risk their capital in endeavors whose demand proves strong will be well-off economically; people in enterprises for which demand proves weak will not do well at all. Luck also plays a role: being born into a family of wealth and education often produces lifelong advantages. And market returns depend critically on well-functioning government institutions, police, civil and criminal courts, laws against fraud and deception, to name but a few. Some substantial portion of the nation's output—of income from both labor and capital—is, therefore, a societal rather than an individual creation. But the returns from that collective enterprise will end up in some individuals' pockets and not in others. In order for this dispersion of economic rewards to be acceptable—for the system to maintain its legitimacy—variations in incomes must be seen to be "fair."

One should never forget that in many ways social insurance to provide reasonable income security is a deeply conservative idea. To be sure, individual motives for supporting the implicit social contract may include feelings of social solidarity, altruism, and obligation. But the great political promoters of social insurance, from Otto von Bismarck to Franklin Roosevelt and beyond, have understood that such guarantees were a necessary feature of a capitalist economy if social harmony and productivity were to be preserved.

Constructing a system that is viewed as fair requires attention to at least four aspects of "fairness." First, the rules of the game must support equal opportunity for all participants. Second, the principle of just deserts must be respected: effort and risk bearing should be rewarded; force, fraud, neglect, and sloth should not. Third, economic risks to income security that are beyond individual control should be buffered by collective action to provide reasonable income security. Those risks include systemwide events or changes (for example, recession, inflation, or rapid technological change), common features of human nature (such as tendencies to discount the future excessively or to undervalue small risks), and personal circumstances like disability, involuntary unemployment, or having been born into an environment of deprivation. Finally, fairness demands progressive financing of collective arrangements to ensure equal opportunity, enforce the rules that preserve just deserts, and share the luck by providing assurances of reasonable income security. Those who benefit most from participation in the economic system should bear the greatest responsibilities for its maintenance.

THE GOALS AND TECHNIQUES OF SOCIAL INSURANCE

The conventional or classic conception of social insurance usually involves a program that is universal, mandatory, wage related, contributory, and publicly administered. In fact, in the United States, only the OASDI program fits that description. Benefits paid pursuant to health insurance policies are not wage related; they are health related. Part B of Medicare, which is rapidly becoming the most important part of that program, is voluntary and only modestly contributory. Workers' compensation is not contributory and is often not publicly administered. Other examples could readily be presented.

Recognizing that most of the social insurance world does not fit this conventional model demonstrates that a host of other programs are directed toward similar goals but use different instruments. Americans make huge public expenditures through tax credits and deductions to support so-called private health insurance and private pensions. There is simply no explanation for these massive subsidies other than a desire to further the goal of family income security in the face of rising and unpredictable health care costs and old age. What should be asked is not whether these programs "count" as social insurance but whether we are getting good value for money in these programs and, if not, how they can be redesigned and reformed.

The question of retirement security, pensions and health care alike, ought to be treated as dependent on both public programs and publicly subsidized private programs. Scholars and policy professionals are beginning to think about how these programs interact and about the necessity of pursuing reform agendas in both domains in order to satisfy basic social insurance goals. The recognition that social insurance is not some set of particular instruments allows for creative thinking about whether measures that are anathema to conventional social insurance advocates might actually do a better job of providing reasonable income security for all Americans.

Pursuing family income security through the tax code may often be a bad idea but not always. And not every "means test" has the same divisive political potential or stigmatizing social effects as conventional public assistance. The earned income tax credit (EITC) is a good example. If tax credits are made refundable and benefits are related to earnings, a tax credit program may provide the best income security protection available today in the United States for low-income families. EITC recipients need not reveal any more about themselves to the Internal Revenue Service, nor in any different form, than their taxpaying neighbors.

It also may mean that using asset accumulation rather than direct transfers will sometimes be an effective technique for providing income security. The past few decades have seen a massive shift in the relative returns to labor and capital in the American economy. Because conventional Social Security pensions are essentially a claim on labor income, there is a case to be made that Americans would be more secure in retirement if their Social Security portfolio included claims on capital assets as well as on the income streams of current workers.

WHAT ABOUT RETIREMENT SECURITY REFORM?

Pensions. Basic public pension guarantees should not be permitted to fall below current levels. Half of current beneficiaries have incomes just exceeding $20,000 per year, and two-thirds of recipients rely on Social Security for most of their income. This means that the redistributive aspect of the current system must be maintained along with its inflation protections.

It does not necessarily mean that the current inflation protections are properly calculated or that Social Security benefits must remain solely dependent on wage income. Establishing some means for providing claims on capital may make sense provided risks are pooled and benefits are not a simple function of individual portfolio investments and returns.

Although the details are not spelled out in William A. Niskanen's paper in this volume (see the next section of this chapter), the Cato Institute proposal does not seem to satisfy these conditions. While average returns may be superior to the current system in that proposal, America is not Lake Wobegon: many Americans will find themselves below average. There is an antipoverty guarantee in the proposal, but this would seem to reintroduce means testing of the old, objectionable sort in a fashion that creates a two-tier system. This guarantee in some sense makes good on the "shared luck" principle of the American social contract, yet it is doubtful that most Americans would agree that it effectively lives up to that ideal.

There also is much more reason to be sanguine about the funding situation of the conventional pension program than Niskanen's paper reveals. Five years ago the system was going into default in 2028; now the deadline has stretched out to 2042. Enacting even a couple of the consensus recommendations from the 1994–96 Advisory Council would close the gap for even longer periods.[1] There is no reason to despair of finding some combination of increased taxes, decreased benefits, and greater returns on endowment that will solve the system's funding problem.

Nor should one imagine that these adjustments are a default on promises or a breach of some rigid intergenerational compact. Adjustment may be necessary in public programs that stretch across decades, indeed, centuries. And there are many ways to share pains and gains from program reform. Furthermore, if Lawrence H. Thompson is correct (see Chapter 7), solving the Social Security and Medicare deficits exclusively by increasing payroll taxes would leave future generations of workers better off financially than this generation and would tend to share the gains and pains of reform equally between workers and retired persons.

Health insurance. Providing family income security against the shocks of large health care costs should be the goal of social insurance. Social insurance is not about reforming medical practice or promoting the public health. Those are laudable goals, but they are goals connected with other policies.

This means that health care insurance should not necessarily promise first-dollar, comprehensive coverage. If people are accustomed to paying "out of pocket" for potato chips and Nintendo games, it is mysterious that copayments and deductibles should become words of scorn for health care insurance proposals. Nor is "catastrophic" coverage unreasonable if properly designed. Michael Graetz and this author made a "catastrophic" proposal several years ago that, if we were right on the numbers, would protect every American family against income insecurity based on high health care costs while spending no more total health care dollars than were already being spent at the time.[2] Maintaining income security for American families while picking up coverage for 41 million uninsured seemed a sensible idea, even though it would necessitate some means testing in order to calibrate the meaning of "catastrophic" with family income.

There is reason for doubt that asset-based strategies for health insurance would be likely to work well. As Dallas Salisbury and his colleagues at the Employee Benefit Research Institute have shown, calculating the assets necessary to meet medical and retirement expenses on an individual basis is virtually impossible.[3] Risk pools of one just do not seem to make much sense where health insurance is involved. Perhaps when the Cato analysts come forward with their promised plan these objections will be overcome, but, if so, those analysts will have been very clever indeed.

The Broader Agenda of Social Security Reform

It is worth pointing out that maintaining income security is a problem that stretches across the life cycle. One may find oneself out of the workforce because of youth and inexperience or because of old age. In the course of a career a worker runs a whole series of risks ranging from individual crises of illness, accident, or layoff to those that result from macroeconomic shifts that devalue earning capacity or that put basic human needs like shelter and health care beyond the means of an earner.

Indeed, income security in old age is the great success story of American social insurance. Forty years ago aged persons were the cohort of the population most likely to be in poverty. Today they are the least likely. On the other hand, nearly one in four children under six lives in a family with an income below poverty level. Moreover, the programs that cushion shocks to income security during working lives are often poorly structured and inadequately funded. There are very limited protections against temporary or partial disability. While unemployment insurance nominally covers 95 percent of American workers, less than 40 percent are likely to find that they are actually eligible for payments during spells of involuntary unemployment. And it is hard to find people who believe that the United States has an effective workers' compensation system. It is only being slightly hyperbolic to say, "find me a person who praises American workers' compensation, and I will show you a lawyer, a consultant, or an expert witness."

Although the pursuit of retirement security is important, there is thus a vast agenda of social insurance reform in the United States that invites attention. And one might well argue that many parts of it are considerably more urgent than the retirement security programs that seem to occupy most of our intellectual energies.

CONCLUSION

When thinking about social insurance and its role in the American social contract, questions of values, goals, and techniques should be separated. It frees the mind to think about the use of novel instruments and to recognize the true nature of the social insurance system in place. In pursuing reasonable income security for all, American goals have been reasonably consistent, but the instruments employed have been highly variable. Since social insurance has been analyzed largely in terms of a specific set of instruments, most have failed to see the connections among diverse programs that are pursuing the same objectives. Staying focused on goals while admitting to flexibility on instruments will not take all of the heat out of social insurance reform debates. But it may shed some light on what the priorities should be and how social insurance can continue to contribute to the realization of a social contract that recognizes the essential importance of both personal responsibility and shared luck.

INCREASING INDIVIDUAL RESPONSIBILITY WOULD IMPROVE RETIREMENT SECURITY

William A. Niskanen

Consideration of the current financial picture of the Social Security, Medicare, and Medicaid programs leads to the conclusion that increasing individual responsibility for retirement income and health care financing would actually bolster retirement security and reduce the cost to future taxpayers. In other words, the Ponzi scheme is over; there is no longer any politically feasible way to maintain retirement and health care security by tax-financed means.

THE LOOMING RETIREMENT CRISIS

Social Security. According to the 2004 annual report of the Social Security trustees, Social Security now faces a net liability of about $12 trillion.[4] Benefits are expected to be higher than tax revenues by 2018, and the trust fund is projected to be exhausted in 2042, after which benefits will have to be reduced by about 27 percent. The tax increases or benefit cuts necessary to put Social Security on a sustainable basis are huge. Either the payroll tax would have to be increased from the current 12.4 percent to 19.4 percent by 2080, an equivalent amount of revenue would have to be raised through other taxes, or benefit provisions would have to be scaled back by an equivalent amount.

The tax increases or benefit reductions necessary to put Social Security on a sustainable basis, however, will not be enough to correct the major biases in the current system. Young workers will earn a rate of return of less than 2 percent, far lower than what they could get in a private retirement account. For workers with the same earnings profile, Social Security is strongly biased against those, such as blacks, with a lower expected life span. And Social Security is most strongly biased against the increasingly prevalent two-worker families because the spousal benefit, equivalent to 50 percent of the retiree's benefit, favors single-earner families, especially those with higher salaries.

Medicare and Medicaid. According to the December 2003 report on "The Long-Term Budget Outlook" by the Congressional Budget Office (CBO), expenditures for Medicare and Medicaid are estimated to increase from 3.9 percent of GDP in 2003 to 11.5 percent in 2050, not even counting the increase in state government expenditures for Medicaid.[5] This may be an optimistic estimate, based on an assumption that annual expenditures per Medicare enrollee will increase only 1 percent a year faster than per capita GDP; in fact, annual expenditures per enrollee have increased 3 percent faster than per capita GDP since 1970, excluding the growth related to demographic changes. If annual expenditures per enrollee increase 2.5 percent faster than per capita GDP, federal expenditures for Medicare and Medicaid alone could be 21.3 percent of GDP by 2050. For comparison, total federal revenues have averaged 18.3 percent of GDP over the past forty years. As the above estimates indicate, the projected increase in federal expenditures for health care is substantially larger than that for Social Security, overwhelms the rest of the federal budget, and will severely limit public tolerance of any tax increase to finance Social Security. Our political system, however, still seems committed to adding to federal medical expenditures, as indicated by the recent approval of prescription drug benefits for the Medicare program and the nearly unanimous endorsement of broader, tax-financed health insurance by the candidates for the Democratic presidential nomination.

Despite the huge increase in the projected federal spending for Medicare and Medicaid, there will still be substantial problems with each program. Both are defined benefit programs, and some potentially desirable treatments are never likely to be covered. Congress has often curtailed the increase in payment rates to providers, a form of price control that limits the access of some Medicare patients to some benefits. Federal matching of state spending for Medicaid makes federal expenditures dependent on the scope of benefits approved by state governments. And, despite the huge outlays for these programs, there are still about 40 million Americans who do not have any health insurance.

SOME SUGGESTED ALTERNATIVES

Social Security. In a July 1998 speech President Clinton acknowledged that the only ways to keep Social Security solvent are to raise taxes, cut benefits, or garner a higher rate of return through private capital investment.[6] In testimony before the Senate in January 1999 Henry Aaron agreed that "increased funding to raise pension reserves is possible only with some combination of additional tax revenues, reduced benefits, or increased investment returns from investing in higher yield assets."[7]

The Cato Institute has been promoting individual, private retirement accounts invested in higher-yield assets as an alternative to Social Security for about twenty-five years. Its distinguished advisory committee on privatization has recently approved a proposal with these provisions:

1. Individuals would be allowed to divert 6.2 percentage points of the payroll tax to privately owned investment accounts. Those choosing to do so would forgo all future accrual of Social Security retirement benefits.

2. The remaining 6.2 percentage points of the payroll tax would be used to fund disability and survivor's benefits and would contribute to funding the transition costs as well.

3. Workers choosing the individual account option would receive a zero-coupon "recognition bond" equal to 95 percent of the accrued value of their lifetime benefits to date. These bonds, redeemable at retirement, would be fully tradable in secondary markets.

4. Contributions to individual accounts would be initially deposited in a balanced fund of 60 percent stocks and 40 percent bonds. Workers would be allowed to choose from a wider array of investment options as the size of their accounts increased.

5. At retirement, workers could choose to purchase an annuity providing yearly income equal to 120 percent of the poverty level, a programmed withdrawal option, or the combination of an annuity and a lump-sum payment.

6. The federal government would provide a safety net ensuring that no worker's retirement income would be below 120 percent of the poverty level. Workers whose accumulations under the private investment option fell below an amount required for purchasing an annuity of that level would receive a supplement sufficient to allow them to do so. This safety net would be financed from general revenues.

7. Those who wished to remain in the traditional Social Security system would be free to do so and would receive a level of retirement benefits payable on a sustainable basis, given the current revenue projections.

The Cato advisory committee proposal includes no explicit provision about how to finance the transition costs above dedicating the remaining 6.2 percent of the payroll tax. Even if this share of the transition costs is financed entirely by a temporary increase in the explicit federal debt, the sum of the explicit debt and the implicit debt of the Social Security program (now about three times the explicit debt) would decline over time with the shrinking number of retirees receiving Social Security benefits.

Medicare and Medicaid. Most policy analysts, including those at Cato, are not yet ready to endorse a specific proposal to deal with the problems of Medicare and Medicaid. The reasons for the extraordinary growth of spending per enrollee are not very clear. The absolute magnitude of the projected expenditures suggests that no conventional reform would prove sufficient. The CBO report, "The Long-Term Budget Outlook," for example, discusses a number of standard options for slowing spending growth and characteristically concludes that ". . . even relatively dramatic policy change would do little to address the long-term fiscal challenge facing Medicare."[8] And there still appears to be broad political support for tax-financed health insurance, at least for the retired and the poor.

An eyes-open perspective on this issue, however, suggests the following:

1. Broad, tax-financed health insurance is part of the problem, not part of the solution. The relative price of medical care has increased much more rapidly since 1965, apparently because an increasing number of people now face lower prices for medical care, principally through third-party payment arrangements. The necessary condition to reduce the growth of tax-financed medical expenditures is that more individuals be exposed to higher prices for medical care.

2. Any tax-financed health insurance should take the form of a defined contribution plan (in which the insured receives a fixed amount of money rather than an open-ended entitlement to benefits) to replace both the Medicare and Medicaid defined benefit plans. Under a defined contribution plan, each individual, not some government agency or insurance company, chooses the treatment option on the advice of his or her physician. An individual's payment for medical care would depend on the price and number of treatments chosen and the plan's deductible and copayment, not on whether the treatment is a covered benefit.

3. Each individual would choose his or her own defined contribution plan, insurance company, and physicians.

4. The primary fiscal support of these plans would be a lump-sum premium subsidy. The amount of this premium subsidy would decline with the individual or household income and increase with the individual's age. The primary fiscal decisions affecting these plans, thus, would be setting the income and age parameters of the premium subsidy. The one tax-financed defined benefit that it is tempting to maintain would be a lump-sum payment for

one physician visit per year, in the expectation that this would reduce the third-party cost of contagious diseases.

As indicated by the general nature of the proposals presented here, there is still a long way to go in the process of working out the details of an alternative to Medicare and Medicaid. And Cato has yet to consider the problems of a transition from the current programs. On one issue, however, the Cato analysts agree: the current programs are fiscally explosive, so it is a matter of urgency to stop adding fuel to the fire.

Enhancing Retirement Security

Social Security. The proposed substitution of individual retirement accounts for Social Security would improve retirement security in several ways:

1. The average real rate of return on the proposed initial portfolio would be about 5 percent, based on the real returns for equities and corporate bonds and the administrative costs now assumed by the Social Security actuaries. This portfolio would be subject to some market risk, depending on the timing of the individual worker's retirement. A study of historical, long-term market returns by the Congressional Research Service, however, found that this portfolio would have outperformed Social Security for the vast bulk of all retirees since the late 1960s and would have earned only slightly less than the average real return to Social Security for the remainder.

2. The average real rate of return on Social Security is estimated to be about 2 percent for workers now age thirty and lower for future workers, assuming payroll taxes are increased to meet the promised benefits. This return, however, is subject to considerable political risk since reluctance to increase taxes may lead to some reduction in the benefits now promised (such as raising the age for full retirement benefits or the scope of the now restricted income tax on future benefits).

3. The individual retirement accounts would have several additional benefits. The rate of return on these accounts would not be biased against those with a shorter expected life span because

any accruals in these accounts upon death would become property of the heirs. The rate of return on these accounts would not be biased against two-worker families, which could lead to greater labor force participation by the lower-wage spouse. And, as private property, these accounts would probably be subject to less political manipulation than promises of the government to which people have no legal claim.

Medicare and Medicaid. The proposed substitution of individual defined contribution health insurance policies for Medicare and Medicaid would enhance retirement security in several ways:

1. Each individual would choose his or her own health insurance plan, insurance company, and physicians. Individuals, on the advice of their physician, would choose the level and frequency of their medical treatments. An increasing number of these choices would no longer be biased by the nature and magnitude of tax-financed health insurance. These conditions would almost surely lead to a more efficient utilization of medical care, a lower rate of increase in the relative price of medical care, and a slower rise in tax-financed expenditures for medical care.

2. In contrast, there is no politically plausible prospect that the federal government would increase taxes by an amount sufficient to finance the indefinite extension of Medicare and Medicaid. As a consequence, the most likely political responses are restrictions on those eligible for these programs, the range of benefits, the approved providers of covered care, and the reimbursement rates of suppliers. Those who continued to be dependent on these programs would face a Soviet-style system of medical care: low quality, long waiting times, and situations in which complaining and political influence are the only ways to obtain satisfactory care.

SUMMARY

There is no longer any acceptable trade-off of further government expenditures for retirement security and no way to bolster retirement security by increasing tax financing of retirement income and health insurance. The most promising way to better retirement security is to promote individual responsibility through major changes in policies that also would reduce the role of government and its outlays.

SOCIAL SECURITY AND THE PRIVATE PENSION SYSTEM

John H. Langbein

This paper examines the policy justifications for Social Security from the perspective of the private pension system. Contrasting Social Security with the private system reveals much about the nature of the public program.

WHAT SOCIAL SECURITY DOES

The distinctive trait of the Social Security system is that it is compulsory. Government power is used to compel workers and employers to contribute. Failure to comply can result in jail time. Social Security entails, therefore, serious infringement of personal liberty. Whenever government interferes with anybody's liberty in a free society, it must be clear about the reasons why; there needs to be justification.

There are two fundamental reasons for the coercion of Social Security: one is paternalistic, the other is redistributive. The paternalistic impulse responds to the simple reality that, without government coercion, large numbers of people will fail to make adequate provision for themselves. Indeed, this was exactly the circumstance in which the Social Security system was born in the 1930s, when the depression left so many elderly people destitute. Even though life expectancies were shorter then and the need for retirement income correspondingly less, not enough people had displayed the foresight and discipline to save adequately for retirement.

The existing private pension system, which promotes personal saving for retirement, has many virtues, but it is a flop when it comes to securing retirement income for those who are least likely to provide for themselves. The private system embraces both traditional defined benefit plans and a range of defined contribution plans or individual account plans: 401(k)s, 403(b)s, 457(b)s, IRAs, profit-sharing plans, and so forth. Although these private plans have assets presently valued at slightly less than $11 trillion, most of that wealth will be delivered to persons in the upper half of the workforce, as measured by income. For the lower half, Social Security will be the only significant source of retirement income.

Social Security can be understood as the successor to a much older "system" of old-age provision, rooted in the family. We all are quite familiar with the process of wealth transfer within the family, from parents to children. Those in the college-tuition-paying phase of life are particularly sensitive to this process. Of old, however, there also was a pattern of reverse wealth transfer, from children to parents, when parents outlived their productive years. Most workers did not live very long after leaving the workforce—they pretty much died with their boots on, so to speak. But when workers (more often their widows) outlived their employment income and had not saved adequately for retirement, they relied upon their children for support. That pattern continues today in less developed countries, where the family is the de facto social security system. Such countries commonly have very high birthrates, at least in part because parents want to have enough children to support them in old age.

The Social Security system effectively superseded this reverse transfer system by collectivizing it and making it mandatory. Government has appropriated the function from the family. Government now taxes the generation of the children to fund transfer payments to the generation of the parents. Intrafamilial wealth transfer now plays virtually no role in the retirement income of the elderly.

This collectivization has many advantages. Because the old system of reverse wealth transfer was limited to the family, persons who were childless, or whose children did not survive, or whose children were unable or unwilling to support them, could be left destitute. By making Social Security mandatory, the government harnessed the earning power of substantially the entire workforce to support the core retirement income needs of the nation's elderly. This attribute of Social Security, universal coverage, is why the program is understood as social insurance. Social Security funds a risk pool that covers persons who, in the days when old-age support was family-based, would not have had assistance. Social Security also has facilitated the growth of our ever more mobile national labor market, freeing workers to locate at great remove from their elderly parents.

The redistributive character of Social Security is closely related to its mandatory nature. Social Security is bottom weighted, meaning that benefit levels as a fraction of earnings are greater for lower-income workers than for higher earners. Social Security benefit levels have largely eliminated poverty among the elderly: at present the poverty rate among the current retiree population at age 67 is only 8 percent. That is a stunning achievement, an important source of American political stability and social peace.

WHAT PRIVATE PENSIONS DO

Proposals to extend individual accounts from the private pension environment into Social Security should provoke concern. The private pension system serves fundamentally different purposes, which would make it difficult to introduce the principles of private retirement provision into Social Security.

In contrast to Social Security's redistributive dynamic, the private system is top weighted; it is skewed to the affluent because its central mechanism is deferral and abatement of income taxes. Three great tax breaks drive the private system. First, taxation of contributions is deferred. The employee does not pay current taxes on sums contributed to his or her pension account, even though these sums are functionally compensation. Rather, the tax bill is deferred for decades, until the worker enters the distribution phase, theoretically in retirement.

Second and even more important is the deferral of income taxes on the investment activity in the account, the so-called buildup. In effect, the pension plan or account receives an interest-free loan from the government in the amount of the deferred taxes on the investment gains. These "borrowed" proceeds compound tax deferred until distribution. This enormous tax benefit is the single most costly subsidy in the entire tax expenditure budget.

The third pension tax break is that when distribution commences upon retirement, the retiree may be in a lower tax bracket than when he or she was employed. The replacement ratio needed to maintain preretirement living standards is usually reckoned at around 70 percent of preretirement income. There are various reasons why: retirees do not pay Social Security and other employment taxes on pension income; they often own their homes free of mortgage; they do not have child-rearing and household-formation expenses; they have a larger personal exemption from the income tax; and much of their health care is publicly provided.

These three pension tax breaks—deferral on contributions, deferral on investment gains, and rate reduction upon distribution—drive the private system. The deep reason why the private system matters so little for the bottom half of the workforce is that those workers have such limited exposure to the income tax. Earners in the bottom half pay Social Security taxes and other employment taxes, and they pay sales and excise taxes, all of which are first-dollar taxes not adjusted to income levels, but they earn so little that the income tax touches them only barely or not at all.

A great maxim would be, "Paupers do not need tax shelters." Therein lies the explanation for why the private pension system as we know it provides virtually no benefits to the poorer half of the workforce.

The private pension system is only incidentally about retirement income. To be sure, private pension plans do and will deliver retirement income to many participants, but in its larger dimension the system is best understood as part of a group of tax shelters that are designed to abate the progressivity of the income tax for the affluent. These shelters include the home mortgage deduction, the exclusion of capital gains on residential housing, the exclusion of employer-paid health insurance, and the favorable treatment of many forms of investment income, including the capital gains rate, forgiveness of capital gains taxation on assets held until death (the so-called stepped-up basis), the exclusion of interest on state and local bonds, and now the lower rate on dividend income.

The net effect of these middle- and upper-middle-class tax shelters is to give the pretense of a moderately progressive tax system but the reality of a flat tax. We Americans do not admit to a flat tax, but in fact most taxpayers pay about a quarter of their income. The status quo serves various interests. It lets politicians on the left brag about having imposed progressive income taxes, and it allows a variety of service providers—lawyers, accountants, actuaries, investment professionals—to enjoy fine incomes from arranging for the affluent to escape much of the bite of these taxes.

This paper spoke earlier of Social Security as the successor to an older pattern of intrafamilial wealth transfer from children to parents.

In this regard, the private pension system offers another striking contrast. More and more of the wealth that is channeled through private pension accounts is being accumulated not for the purpose of providing retirement income but for discretionary savings and for intergenerational wealth transfer to children and grandchildren. The use of pension accounts as tax-favored savings, investment, and wealth transmission devices is possible only in the defined contribution system, in which the participant builds an individual account, whose unexpended proceeds can be accessed for nonretirement purposes or left to transferees. In a 401(k) or 403(b) plan or an IRA, the participant can cash out in whole or in part at any time (free of penalty after age fifty-nine and a half). If the participant or spouse leaves unexpended proceeds at death, the minimum distribution rules allow heirs or other transferees to perpetuate the tax shelter for many years as they draw down the account. These attributes of individual account plans have been a major attraction in the notable shift from defined benefit to defined contribution plans that has been going on in the private system over the past two decades. Defined benefit plans typically pay retirement income only, and only for the participant and spouse. If they die early, the shortening of the payment obligation benefits the plan sponsor, not their heirs.

The very term "pension plan" is increasingly a misnomer for defined contribution plans. They are in truth multipurpose savings, investment, and wealth transmission vehicles for the tax-sensitive classes.

SUMMARY

The differences in purpose between Social Security and the private system, especially the individual account plans that are now so prevalent, are profound. Whereas Social Security is compulsory and redistributive, participation in the private system is largely voluntary and wholly devoid of any redistributive component. Whereas Social Security is bottom weighted, favoring those less well-off, the private system is top weighted, delivering most of its benefit in the form of tax advantages attractive only to upper-bracket taxpayers. In view of these stark functional differences, the likelihood that the private system could be a model for the reform of Social Security seems remote.

7.

PAYING FOR RETIREMENT
SHARING THE GAIN

Lawrence H. Thompson

INTRODUCTION

The aging of the baby-boom generation will increase the cost of providing health care and income support to our elderly population. These higher costs will reduce future living standards, at least relative to the situation in the absence of any demographic shift. The exact impact on the living standards of future workers and retirees will depend on the pace and pattern of future economic growth, the particular adjustments made to finance Social Security and Medicare, and trends in the cost and volume of the health services consumed.

Economic prosperity creates resources to accommodate the increased cost. If growth is sufficiently rapid, it will be possible both to finance the baby boom's retirement and to allow future workers and retirees to enjoy gradually rising standards of living. Strong economic expansion does not itself ensure this result, however. The impact on the living standards of discrete groups also will depend on how the "growth dividend" is shared and how the costs of adjusting Social Security and Medicare are apportioned.

The economic growth rates currently projected by the trustees of Social Security and Medicare are sufficient to accommodate the cost of the baby boom's retirement without forcing reductions from current living standards on either workers or retirees in generations to come. However, current policies are likely to lift the living standards of future workers by substantially more than those of future Social Security beneficiaries. The gap between the impact on workers and retirees is large enough that a payroll tax rate increase could be used to restore financial balance to both Social Security and Medicare without disadvantaging those still in the labor force.

Relying on tax rate increases to finance the baby boom's retirement raises questions about generational equity. Nevertheless, even if payroll taxes were increased, the present value of the financial flows from parents to children in a child's early years would probably exceed the present value of the payroll tax payments that the child would be asked to make over his or her subsequent working life.

DISTRIBUTING THE GAINS OF ECONOMIC GROWTH

As a matter of principle, Congress has favored distributing the gains from economic growth and the pain associated with Social Security financing reforms more or less equally between workers and beneficiaries. It considered explicitly how Social Security benefits should be adjusted to real wage increases when the current benefit indexing rules were adopted in 1977. At that point it decided that initial benefit levels should increase over time at the same rate as average earnings levels increased.[1] Six years later, the reforms recommended by the Greenspan Commission to restore short-range financial stability were advertised as representing a balanced approach that shared the pain of restructuring roughly equally between workers and beneficiaries. Of the financing changes made between 1983 and 1989, 50 percent were from payroll tax increases, 40 percent were from benefit reductions, and 10 percent involved accelerating previously scheduled general fund payments.[2]

Although in each case Congress acted with the objective of sharing pain and gain equitably, current policies appear to be producing a different result. Future beneficiaries are likely not to enjoy increased living standards to the same degree as workers. The primary reason for this is the incomplete coverage of the health benefits offered to the aged under Medicare, even after the enactment of the prescription drug benefit. The income tax treatment of Social Security benefits and the phased increase in the retirement age also contribute.

The analysis of the impact of current trends is shown in Table 7.1 (see page 118). Data taken largely from the most recent Social Security and Medicare trustees' reports are used to analyze the change in the living standards of hypothetical workers and beneficiaries under the trustees' long-range assumptions. Living standards are measured by income after deducting out-of-pocket health spending and adjusting for any increase in the taxes needed to finance Social Security and Medicare.

The calculations begin by tracking trends in living standards for the hypothetical worker with average earnings. Under current assumptions, average earnings are projected to grow between 2003 and 2030 by 35 percent after inflation. Since no changes are currently scheduled in the employee payroll tax rate, the net wage after social insurance contributions also will grow by 35 percent.

Three developments related to health spending are expected to absorb some of these gains, however. First, the trustees project that Supplementary Medical Insurance (SMI) expenditures will rise substantially faster than GDP over this period of time, and three-quarters of the cost will have to be met from general fund taxes. Second, although workers have fewer out-of-pocket health costs than retirees, persons under age sixty-five still devote some 4 percent of their before-tax income to health, and these expenditures are likely to rise more rapidly than average earnings. Finally, the prescription drug program that was just enacted further increases health spending on Medicare beneficiaries that will be financed from the general fund. The estimated impact of the first two of these is shown in the first set of calculations in Table 7.1, while the estimated impact of the prescription drug benefit is shown further down in the table. Higher out-of-pocket spending and the increased income taxes needed to finance SMI absorb three percentage points of the projected increase in net earnings, leaving the average worker with a 32 percent increase in living standards.

The prospects for a typical beneficiary who is retiring after a career as an average earner are far less promising. The trustees predict that such a beneficiary retiring at the normal retirement age in 2030 can expect a benefit some 35 percent higher than that received by the average earner in 2003, which is the same as the percentage

TABLE 7.1. PROJECTED AVERAGE EARNINGS AND AVERAGE SOCIAL SECURITY BENEFITS (THOUSANDS OF 2003 DOLLARS UNDER 2003 TRUSTEES' REPORT ASSUMPTIONS)

	2003	2030	PERCENTAGE CHANGE
CURRENT PATH (BEFORE PRESCRIPTION BENEFIT)			
Average Worker			
1. Gross average wage	34,731	46,903	35
2. Less: employee Social Security tax	2,657	3,588	
3. Net wage	32,074	43,315	35
4. Less: income tax increase to finance increase in SMI		472	
5. Wage net of SMI tax increase	32,074	42,843	34
6. Less: out-of-pocket health spending	1,472	2,416	
7. Wage net of Social Security taxes and health spending	30,601	40,427	32
Average Beneficiary			
8. Benefit at normal retirement age	13,970	18,860	35
9. Benefit at age sixty-five	13,814	16,345	18
10. Less: SMI premium	704	1,305	
11. Net benefit received	13,110	15,040	15
12. Less: Medicare cost sharing	1,028	1,599	
13. Less: other out-of-pocket spending	2,083	3,504	
14. Benefit net of health spending	9,999	9,937	-1
15. Less: income tax on Social Security benefits		173	
16. Less: income tax increase to finance increase in SMI		59	
17. Benefit less tax and health spending increases	9,999	9,705	-3
ESTIMATED IMPACT OF PRESCRIPTION DRUG BENEFIT			
Workers			
18. Additional income tax to pay benefit		335	
19. Revised wage net of tax increases and health spending	30,601	40,092	31
Beneficiaries			
20. Reduction in out-of-pocket health spending		1,372	
21. Increase in income taxes to finance		43	
22. Revised net benefit	9,999	11,034	10
23. Annuity value of net benefit (x1,000)	143.9	170.1	18
IMPACT OF PAYROLL TAX INCREASE TO BALANCE PROGRAMS			
24. Cost of 6.5 percentage point increase in payroll tax		3,049	
25. Revised net wage	30,601	37,044	21

Sources:

Row 1: Trustees' Report of the Federal Old-Age and Survivors Insurance and Disability Insurance Trust Funds, Social Security Administration, 2003 Annual Report, Tables V.C1 and VI.F7.

Row 2: .0765 times #1.

Row 4: 75 percent of the increase in SMI expenditures as a percentage of GDP, divided by the ratio of total wages (as reported on income tax returns) to GDP, multiplied by the ratio of the average tax rate among households in the $30,000 to $40,000 income range (8 percent) to the average tax rate across all households (15 percent), multiplied by the projected wage. Data from Boards of Trustees of the Hospital Insurance and Supplementary Medical Insurance Trust Funds, Centers for Medicare and Medicaid Services, 2003 Annual Report, Table II.A3, and Statistics of Income, Historical Data, release of Summer 2003, Tables 1 and 3.

Row 6: 2003 spending based on 1988 Consumer Expenditure Survey, Table 4500; the 1988 data were used to derive an estimate of out-of-pocket spending for 2000; the fraction of family income devoted to such spending in 1988 was multiplied by the average earnings figure for 2000; out-of-pocket spending among workers was projected to grow after 2000 at the same rate as out-of-pocket spending for the aged.

Rows 8 and 9: Trustees' Report of the Federal Old-Age and Survivors Insurance and Disability Insurance Trust Funds, Social Security Administration, 2003 Annual Report, Table VI.F11.

Row 10: Boards of Trustees of the Hospital Insurance and Supplementary Medical Insurance Trust Funds, Centers for Medicare and Medicaid Services, 2003 Annual Report, Table II.C2, increased to 2030 by the percentage increase in SMI expenditures per SMI enrollee.

Rows 12 and 13: Stephanie Maxwell, Marilyn Moon, and Misha Segal, "Growth in Medicare and Out-of-Pocket Spending: Impact on Vulnerable Beneficiaries," Urban Institute, Washington, D.C., 2001. Projections extended from 2025 to 2030 and updated based on the percentage change in projected per enrollee Medicare spending for each future year between the 2000 and 2003 reports.

Row 15: One-half of the difference between the projected 2030 benefit (in nominal dollars) and the taxation threshold that year, multiplied by the average tax rate for individuals and households in the $9,000 to $11,000 income range (3 percent).

Row 16: Similar to row 4, except using the average tax rate for households in the $9,000 to $11,000 range instead of the $30,000 to $40,000 range.

Row 18: Similar to row 4, except that the additional taxes needed to finance the benefit are derived from CBO estimates of total outlays as of 2010; these were expressed as a percentage of GDP and assumed to grow at the same rate as total out-of-pocket spending of aged individuals.

Row 20: CBO projection of 2010 spending on the drug benefit adjusted to 2003 dollars and divided by the projected total 2010 Medicare enrollment.

Row 21: Similar to row 18, except with the lower average tax rate.

Row 23: Annuity factors assume two-thirds joint and survivor annuity based on male and female mortality tables that had the age sixty-five life expectancy assumed by the trustees for each year.

Row 24: 6.5 percent of the gross wage.

increase projected for average earnings. However, because the increase in the normal retirement age means progressively larger reductions in benefits taken before the normal retirement age, the benefit for the average earner retiring at age sixty-five in 2030 will be only 18 percent higher than the benefit awarded a similar retiree at the same age in 2003.

The gain in beneficiary living standards is further eroded by the projected increases in their health spending. Assuming that the SMI premium grows at the same rate as SMI spending per enrolled beneficiary, it will double between now and 2030 and absorb three percentage points of the growth in benefits.[3] The impact of other out-of-pocket spending is even more dramatic. The figures shown in Table 7.1 use recent estimates prepared at the Urban Institute as a basis for calculating these other out-of-pocket expenditures.[4] They are projected to rise by more than 60 percent between 2003 and 2030, sufficiently large to absorb all of the remaining real benefit increase. After deducting anticipated out-of-pocket health spending, the real net benefit for the hypothetical retiree in question is projected to drop by 1 percent between 2003 and 2030.

Two other small changes cause a further fall in real net benefits. Retirees will have to share a portion of the tax burden of the increased general fund subsidy for the SMI program, although their lower incomes mean that they pay substantially less than workers. Future beneficiaries will have to pay income taxes on a rising fraction of their Social Security benefits as well since the tax-exempt threshold is fixed in nominal terms. Under the trustees' assumptions, inflation will halve the real value of the tax-exempt threshold between 2003 and 2030.

The net effect of these final two adjustments is to subtract another 2 percent from 2030 net benefits. The combination of soaring health expenditures, rising income tax burdens (partially associated with the jump in health expenditures), and the increments in the normal retirement age eliminates all of the increase in retiree living standards that might have been envisioned when the 1977 amendments were adopted.

There are at least two important qualifiers to this rather bleak assessment. First, the prescription drug benefit just enacted will significantly ease beneficiary out-of-pocket health spending and will allow the hypothetical beneficiary tracked here to avoid an absolute decline in living standards. Second, thus far the analysis has focused only on monthly benefits and has ignored the projected increase in life expectancy.

The third and fourth sets of numbers in Table 7.1 add estimates of the impact of the prescription drug benefit to the analysis. The reduction in out-of-pocket spending shown here is simply the aggregate outlays for the drug benefit as projected by the Congressional Budget Office for the year 2010 divided by projected Medicare enrollment that year. This figure is then modified using the same rate of growth as other out-of-pocket spending between 2010 and 2030. The resulting estimate suggests that the prescription drug bill will reduce out-of-pocket spending for the average retiree by about 20 percent. Taking into consideration the modest amount of additional general fund taxes that such a retiree will have to pay to help finance this benefit, the net effect is to raise the projected gain in living standards between 2003 and 2030 to some 10 percent. Deducting the higher income taxes that workers will have to pay to finance this benefit reduces their gain to some 31 percent. At this point, the hypothetical worker can still look forward to an increase in living standards that is three times the increase that his or her beneficiary counterpart can anticipate.

Longer life expectancy counters the effect of later retirement. The trustees assume that life expectancy at age sixty-five will be extended by 1.8 years between 2003 and 2030, increasing the annuity value of any given monthly benefit. In this case, the longer life expectancy causes the 10 percent increase in the net monthly benefit calculated above to translate into an 18 percent increase in the annuity value of the benefit package.

The final set of numbers in Table 7.1 explores the impact on workers of closing the financing gap currently projected for Social Security and Medicare entirely through increases in payroll tax rates. The estimate calls for a 6.5 percentage point hike, roughly equivalent to the 2035 shortfall in Social Security and Hospital Insurance combined. It presumes that workers pay the entire 6.5 percentage point increase, as would be the case if the employers' share were shifted entirely onto workers in the form of lower wages. Even with that kind of tax increase, the average earner's income after tax and health spending would rise by 21 percent. This would still afford future workers twice the 10 percent increase that future beneficiaries could expect in their net monthly benefits. It is roughly equivalent to the 18 percent increase in the annuity value of the average net benefit.

INTERGENERATIONAL TRANSFERS:
ARE PAYROLL TAXES FAIR?

Social Security is frequently analyzed as if it were a program of mandatory, individual retirement savings accounts whose most important attribute was the rate of return earned on past contributions. The program also can be appropriately characterized, however, as an intergenerational compact that socializes the traditional responsibility of children to take care of their elderly parents. Institutionalizing this responsibility makes retirement incomes more secure and obligations more enforceable, spreads the cost of supporting the elderly more equitably across the income distribution, preserves the dignity of both beneficiaries and contributors, and integrates old-age protection with disability and survivor protection.

Social Security is only half of the traditional pattern of intergenerational transfers, however; the other half is made up of the transfers that flow from parents to children within each family, particularly when the children are young. An appropriate way of assessing Social Security's impact on net intergenerational transfers is to compare the magnitude of these two financial flows.

Using data from the 1990–92 Consumer Expenditure Survey, Mark Lino estimates that in 1998 a middle-income family of four spent an average of $8,705 per year on each child, out of a mean pretax income of $47,900, and that a high-income family spent an average of $12,705 per child per year, out of a mean pretax income of $90,700. These estimates form the basis for the calculations in Table 7.2.

Under the trustees' economic assumptions, Lino's estimates suggest that parents will transfer resources with a present value (in 1998 prices) of some $154,000 by the time a child reaches age eighteen.[5] If one assumes that the child born into the higher-income household is dependent through age twenty-two and goes to a college that requires additional outlays of $15,000 a year (1998 prices), the present value of the parental transfers comes to $268,000.

Table 7.2 compares the present value of the parent-to-child transfers to the present value of the payroll taxes that the children in these households can expect to pay. The children are the cohort born in 1998 and are likely to work into the decade of the 2060s. In each case, tax payments include both the employer and employee share of Social Security and Medicare payroll taxes, and the tax rates are set at whatever is needed to cover each year's total expenditures for all

Table 7.2. Estimated Intrafamily Transfers, Illustrative Average and High-Income Families (1998 birth cohort; 1998 dollars; 2003 Trustees' Report assumptions)

		Average Income	High Income
1.	Average family income	$47,900	$90,700
2.	Transfers from parents to child (present value)		
	3. Costs of raising child	160,271	276,572
	4. College tuition		47,181
	5. Subtotal: transfers to succeeding generation	160,271	323,764
6.	Transfers from child to parent (present value)		
	7. Social Security and Medicare taxes, current rates	107,459	240,361
	8. Additional taxes to finance shortfall	25,311	69,358
	9. Subtotal: transfers to preceding generation	132,770	309,719
10.	Net transfer to subsequent generation	27,501	14,035

Sources:

Row 3: Estimate of 1998 costs from Mark Lino, "Expenditures on Children by Families" (Miscellaneous Publication no. 1528-1998), *1998 Annual Report,* Center for Nutrition Policy and Promotion, U.S. Department of Agriculture, 1999, increased each year by the rate of growth of average earnings that year and discounted back to 1998 by the government bond rate; earnings growth and government bond rates are from the Trustees' Report of the Federal Old-Age and Survivors Insurance and Disability Insurance Trust Funds, Social Security Administration, 2003 Annual Report.

Row 4: $15,000 in 1998, increased for subsequent years at the rate of growth of average earnings and discounted back to 1998 by the government bond rate.

Row 5: 15.3 percent of the average (or maximum taxable) earnings under Social Security each year as projected in the Trustees' Report of the Federal Old-Age and Survivors Insurance and Disability Insurance Trust Funds, Social Security Administration, 2003 Annual Report, discounted by the government bond rate.

Row 6: Projected average (or maximum) wage multiplied by the additional combined employer-employee rate required to cover the current costs of the Social Security and Hospital Insurance/Supplemental Medical Insurance programs in years after the respective trust funds are projected to be exhausted.

years after the currently projected exhaustion date of the respective trust funds. The individual from the middle-income household is assumed to work for forty-three years at the average wage. The individual from the high-income household starts work a little later and works a little longer, ending up with forty-two years of work, all of them at the maximum taxable earnings level.

These explorations find that the present value of the initial transfer from the parents to the children in a typical middle-income household is likely to be comfortably above the present value of the transfers (in the form of future payroll taxes) from the children to the parents, even if payroll tax rates are increased to close the Social Security and Medicare financing gaps. The gap between the size of the parent-to-child transfer and the size of the subsequent child-to-parent transfer is large enough that extending the analysis to include the child's contribution to the SMI program is not likely to change the result.

Even the child of the high-income household is a net recipient of intergenerational transfers when only the payroll tax is considered, although the gap is substantially smaller. For the high-wage worker, though, extending the analysis to include the taxes used to finance the SMI program would clearly tip the flow of resources toward the parents and away the child. However, this may be taken more as an indication of the progressive nature of the tax and transfer arrangement than as evidence of an intergenerational imbalance.

SHARING THE BURDEN

The pace of economic growth assumed in the current official cost projections is sufficient to allow future workers and retirees to enjoy higher living standards, even after the adjustments needed to finance the retirement of the baby-boom generation. Current Social Security and Medicare policies are not likely to result in an equitable distribution of the net gains from economic expansion, however, at least not in the manner envisioned by the Congress when it set up the current benefit indexing rules in 1977.

The combination of recent and projected health care cost trends and the income tax changes adopted in 1983 could eliminate all growth in net retirement benefits (benefits net of both taxes and health costs) over the next thirty years. In contrast, workers can look forward to continued increases in living standards over these years. Current policies are placing the cost of adjusting to the retirement of the baby-boom generation disproportionately on future retirees.

The recent prescription drug benefit will narrow but not eliminate the differential between the gains that future workers and future retirees can expect. The gap separating the two groups' aggregate well-being after that program is implemented is likely to be large enough that the entire shortfall in both Social Security and Hospital Insurance could be closed through payroll tax rate increases without disadvantaging workers relative to beneficiaries.

The added burden of the payroll tax rate increases that would be needed to finance Social Security and Medicare over the next sixty to sixty-five years also does not appear unreasonable when compared to the size of the intergenerational flows of resources between parents and children that occur within a typical family. Most children would still be net recipients of intergenerational transfers even if they had to pay more in future payroll taxes to support the retirement of their parents' generation.

NOTES

CHAPTER 2

1. Richard W. Johnson, "Changing the Age of Medicare Eligibility: Implications for Older Adults, Employers, and the Government," Urban Institute, Washington, D.C., December 2003, p. 34, available online at http://www.urban.org/UploadedPDF/410902_changing_age_medicare.pdf.

2. David M. Cutler, "Declining Disability among the Elderly," *Health Affairs* 20, no. 6 (November/December 2001): 11–27.

3. David T. Ellwood, "The Sputtering Labor Force of the 21st Century: Can Social Policy Help?" NBER Working Paper no. w8321, National Bureau of Economic Research, Cambridge, Mass., June 2001, pp. 3–20, available online at http://papers.nber.org/papers/w8321.pdf.

4. Ibid.

5. "New Opportunities for Older Workers," a Statement by the Research and Policy Committee of the Committee for Economic Development, New York, October 1999, pp. 10–12, available online at http://www.ced.org/docs /report/report_older.pdf; Deborah Parkinson, "Voices of Experience: Mature Workers in the Future Workforce," Report no. R-1319-02-RR, Conference Board, New York, November 2002.

6. Stephanie Maxwell, Marilyn Moon, and Misha Segal, "Growth in Medicare and Out-of-Pocket Spending: Impact on Vulnerable Beneficiaries," report, Commonwealth Fund, New York, January 2001, pp. 14–16, available online at http://www.cmwf.org/usr_doc/maxwell_increases_430.pdf.

7. The range is determined by various assumptions regarding longevity, premiums, and out-of-pocket expenses. Paul Fronstin and Dallas Salisbury, "Retiree Health Benefits: Savings Needed to Fund Health Care in Retirement," EBRI Issue Brief no. 254, Employee Benefit Research Institute, Washington, D.C., February 2003, pp. 1–14, available online at http://www.ebri.org/pdfs/0203ib.pdf.

8. Ibid.

9. Edward N. Wolff, "The Devolution of the American Pension System: Who Gained and Who Lost?" paper delivered at National Academy of Social Insurance 16th Annual Conference, January 22–23, 2004, Washington, D.C., January 2004.

10. With a 5 percent annual return and new contributions equal to 10 percent of pay, the fund would grow to about $210,000. See the "Projecting Your Account Balance" menu option (under "Calculators") for FERS (Federal Employees' Retirement System) participants on the Web site of the Thrift Savings Plan, available online at http://www.tsp.gov/calc/PAB_intro.html.

11. Assuming interest rates and other annuity terms remained the same.

CHAPTER 3

1. Dora L. Costa, *The Evolution of Retirement: An American Economic History, 1880–1990* (Chicago: University of Chicago Press, 1998), pp. 6–9.

2. Robert L. Clark et al., *The Economics of an Aging Society* (Oxford: Blackwell Publishing, 2004), Chapter 10.

3. "The Retirement Prospects of the Baby Boomers," Economic and Budget Issue Brief, Congressional Budget Office, March 18, 2004, available online at http://www.cbo.gov/showdoc.cfm?index=5195&sequence=0.

4. John Maynard Keynes, "Economic Possibilities for Our Grandchildren," in *The Collected Writing of John Maynard Keynes,* vol. 9, *Essays in Persuasion* (New York: St. Martin's Press, 1972), pp. 332–34.

5. David T. Ellwood, "Winners and Losers in America: Taking the Measure of the New Economic Realities," in David T. Ellwood et al., *A Working Nation: Workers, Work, and Government in the New Economy* (New York: Russell Sage Foundation Publications, 2000), pp. 1–41.

6. Lawrence Mishel, Jared Bernstein, and John Schmitt, *The State of Working America,* 2000/2001 (Ithaca, N.Y.: Cornell University Press, 2001).

7. Kevin Phillips, *Wealth and Democracy: A Political History of the American Rich* (New York: Broadway Books, 2002), p. 63.

8. Donald O. Parsons, "The Decline in Male Labor Force Participation," *Journal of Political Economy* 88, no. 1 (February 1980): 117–34; Alan L. Gustman and Thomas L. Steinmeier, "Partial Retirement and the Analysis of Retirement Behavior," *Industrial and Labor Relations Review* 37, no. 3 (April 1984): 403–15; Alan L. Gustman and Thomas L. Steinmeier, "The 1983 Social Security Reforms and Labor Supply Adjustments of Older Individuals in the Long Run," *Journal of Labor Economics* 3, no. 2 (April 1985): 237–53; Michael V. Leonesio, Denton R. Vaughn, and Bernard

Wixon, "Early Retirees under Social Security: Health Status and Economic Resources," *Social Security Bulletin* 63, no. 4 (September 2001): 1–16. An earlier, working paper version is available online at http://www.ssa.gov/policy /docs/workingpapers/wp86.pdf.

9. John P. Robinson and Geoffrey Godbey, *Time for Life: The Surprising Ways Americans Use Their Time* (State College, Pa.: Pennsylvania State University Press, 1997), pp. 214–16.

10. John W. Rowe and Robert L. Kahn, *Successful Aging: The MacArthur Foundation Study Shows You How the Lifestyle Choices You Make Now— More than Heredity—Determine Your Health and Vitality* (New York: Pantheon, 1998), pp. 173–77.

11. Robert M. Hutchens, "Delayed Payment Contracts and a Firm's Propensity to Hire Older Workers," *Journal of Labor Economics* 4, no. 4 (October 1986): 439-57.

12. See David Neumark, "Age Discrimination Legislation in the United States," NBER Working Paper no. w8152, National Bureau of Economic Research, Cambridge, Mass., March 2001, available online at http://papers.nber.org/papers/w8152.pdf, for a review of the age discrimination literature.

13. Kevin D. Neuman, "Does Retirement Affect the Health of Older Workers? Evidence from the Health and Retirement Study," working paper, University of Notre Dame, 2003.

14. Elizabeth Arias, "United States Life Tables, 2000," *National Vital Statistics Reports* (National Center for Health Statistics, Centers for Disease Control and Prevention, Hyattsville, Md.) 51, no. 3 (December 19, 2002), available online at http://www.cdc.gov/nchs/data/nvsr/nvsr51/nvsr51_03.pdf.

15. *Statistical Abstract of the United States 2002: The National Data Book,* Bureau of the Census, U.S. Department of Commerce, Table 621, p. 406.

16. Neal Weinberg, "Help Wanted: Older Workers Need Not Apply," CNN.com, September 14, 1998, available online at http://www.cnn.com /TECH/computing/9809/14/tooold.idg/.

17. Congressional Budget Office, "Baby Boomers' Retirement Prospects: An Overview," 2004, available online at http://www.cbo.gov/ftpdocs/48xx/doc4863 /11-26-BabyBoomers.pdf; Alicia H. Munnell, "The Declining Role of Social Security," *Just the Facts on Retirement Issues* (Center for Retirement Research at Boston College), no. 6, February 2003, available online at http://www.bc.edu /centers/crr/facts/jtf_6.pdf.

18. Premium costs for a single man in his sixties are twice as high as for a single man in his forties; family premiums for a worker in his early sixties are more than four times as high as individual premiums for a worker in his early forties. (Statistics from Hewitt Health Value Initiative [Lincolnshire, Ill.: Hewitt Associates, 1995], cited in Virginia Reno and June Eichner, "Ensuring Health and Income Security for an Aging Workforce," National

Academy of Social Insurance. Brief No. 1, December 2000, available online at http://www.nasi.org/usr_doc/risks_brief_1.pdf.) And premiums for employer-sponsored health insurance rose by 13.9 percent in 2003, the third straight year of double-digit increases and the largest growth in a single year since 1990, according to a national survey of employers ("Employer Health Benefits, Annual Survey 2003," Henry J. Kaiser Family Foundation and Health Research and Educational Trust, Washington, D.C., October 2003, available online at http://www.kff.org/insurance /ehbs2003-1-set.cfm).

19. Frank McArdle et al., *The Current State of Retiree Health Benefits: Findings from the Kaiser/Hewitt 2002 Retiree Health Survey,* Henry J. Kaiser Family Foundation, Menlo Park, Calif., and Hewitt Associates, Lincolnshire, Ill., December 2002, pp. 9–16, available online at http://www.kff.org/medicare /loader.cfm?url=/commonspot/security/getfile.cfm&PageID=14031.

20. Retiree health benefits bridge the gap between early retirement and entitlement to Medicare at age sixty-five and usually wrap around Medicare after sixty-five. About one in three elderly have this supplemental coverage (William J. Wiatrowski, "Retiree Health Care Benefits: Data Collection Issues," Bureau of Labor Statistics, July 29, 2003, available online at http://www.bls.gov/opub/cwc/cm20030711ar01p1.htm). Large companies introduced the benefits in the 1940s, 1950s, and 1960s, when business was booming and active workers greatly outnumbered retirees. In the past ten to fifteen years, three developments led companies to change retiree health benefits. First, their retiree populations grew much faster than their active workers. Second, health costs per retiree rose rapidly. Finally, new accounting standards issued in 1990 called on companies to show their future retiree health obligations on their financial statements (see Paul Fronstin and Virginia Reno, "Recent Trends in Retiree Benefits and the Role of COBRA Coverage," Health and Income Security for an Aging Workforce Brief no. 4, National Academy of Social Insurance, Washington, D.C., June 2001, available online at http://www.nasi.org/usr_doc/risks_brief_4.pdf).

21. Clark et al., *Economics of Aging,* p. 23.

22. "Disability Characteristics of Persons 16 to 74," Current Population Survey, Bureau of the Census, U.S. Department of Commerce, 2002, available online at http://www.census.gov/hhes/www/disable/cps/cps102.htm.

23. Leora Friedberg, "The Impact of Technological Change on Older Workers: Evidence from Data on Computer Use," NBER Working Paper no. 8297, National Bureau of Economic Research, Cambridge, Mass., May 2001, available online at http://papers.nber.org/papers/w8297.pdf.

24. Luojia Hu, "The Hiring Decisions and Compensation Structures of Large Firms," *Industry and Labor Relations Review* 56, no. 4 (July 2003): 663, reprint available online at http://faculty.econ.northwestern.edu/faculty /hu/FirmILRR0703.pdf; Hutchens, "Delayed Payment Contracts."

25. Anne C. Case and Angus Deaton, "Broken Down by Work and Sex: How Our Health Declines," NBER Working Paper no. w9821, National Bureau of Economic Research, Cambridge, Mass., July 2003, available online at http://papers.nber.org/papers/w9821.pdf; Randall K. Filer and Peter A. Petri, "A Job-Characteristics Theory of Retirement," *Review of Economics and Statistics* 70, no. 1 (February 1988): 123–29.

26. "Worker Displacement, 1999–2001," news release, Bureau of Labor Statistics, U.S. Department of Labor, August 21, 2002, available online at ftp://ftp.bls.gov/pub/news.release/History/disp.08212002.news.

27. Richard W. Johnson and David B. Neumark, "Age Discrimination, Job Separations, and Employment Status of Older Workers: Evidence from Self-Reports," *Journal of Human Resources* 32, no. 4 (Fall 1997): 779–811; John Fountain, "Age Counts in Hiring, the Older Jobless Find," *New York Times,* November 13, 2002, p. A16, available online at http://www.globalaging.org /elderrights/us/hiring.htm.

28. Fountain, "Age Counts in Hiring."

29. Steven Hipple, "Worker Displacement in the Mid-1990s," *Monthly Labor Review* 122, no. 7 (July 1999): 15–32.

30. Teresa Ghilarducci and Kevin Neuman, "The Distribution of Early Retirement Leisure: Evidence from the Health and Retirement Study," unpublished paper, University of Notre Dame, 2004.

31. John R. Wolfe, "Perceived Longevity and Early Retirement," *Review of Economics and Statistics* 65, no. 4 (November 1983): 544–51.

32. Filer and Petri, "Job-Characteristics Theory of Retirement."

33. Eric Lofgren, Steven Nyce, and Sylvester Schieber, "Designing Total Reward Packages for Tight Labor Markets," in Olivia S. Mitchell et al., eds., *Benefits for the Workplace of the Future* (Philadelphia: University of Pennsylvania Press, 2003), pp. 149–77.

CHAPTER 4

1. Calculated from national income accounts data published on the Web site of the Organization for Economic Cooperation and Development, Paris, available online at http://www.oecd.org.

2. Robert Wuthnow, *Poor Richard's Principle: Recovering the American Dream through the Moral Dimension of Work, Business, and Money* (Princeton, N.J.: Princeton University Press, 1996), p. 6.

3. Douglas B. Bernheim, Jonathan Skinner, and Steven Weinberg, "What Accounts for the Variation in Retirement Wealth among U.S. Households?" *American Economic Review* 91, no. 4 (September 2001): 832–57.

4. Richard H. Thaler and H. M. Shefrin, "An Economic Theory of Self-Control," *Journal of Political Economy* 89, no. 2 (April 1981): 392–406.

5. George Ainslie, *Picoeconomics: The Strategic Interaction of Successive Motivational States within the Person* (New York: Cambridge University Press, 1992), Chapter 3.

6. For an extensive summary of this evidence, see Robert H. Frank, *Choosing the Right Pond: Human Behavior and the Quest for Status* (New York: Oxford University Press, 1985), Chapter 2.

7. Melvin Konner, *The Tangled Wing: Biological Constraints on the Human Spirit* (New York: Holt, Rinehart and Winston, 1982).

8. People who report that they are not happy, for example, are more likely to experience headaches, rapid heartbeat, digestive disorders, and related ailments. Those who rate themselves as very happy are more likely than others to initiate social contacts with friends. For a more detailed survey of this evidence, see Robert H. Frank, *Luxury Fever: Why Money Fails to Satisfy in an Era of Excess* (New York: Free Press, 1999), Chapters 5 and 7.

9. Larry M. Bartels, "Homer Gets a Tax Cut: Inequality and Public Policy in the American Mind," paper presented at the Annual Meeting of the American Political Science Association, Philadelphia, August 2003, available online at http://www.brookings.edu/dybdocroot/comm/events/20031216_Bartels.pdf.

10. See Frank, *Choosing the Right Pond,* Chapter 8. The patterns are: (1) as income grows over time, savings rates remain roughly constant; (2) consumption is more stable over time than income; and (3) high-income individuals save at greater rates than those with lower incomes.

11. Robert H. Frank and Phillip J. Cook, *The Winner-Take-All Society* (New York: The Free Press, 1995).

12. For a survey, see Frank, *Choosing the Right Pond,* Chapter 2.

13. "Construction and Housing," Statistical Abstract of the United States 2002: The National Data Book, Bureau of the Census, U.S. Department of Commerce, 2003, section 20, available online at http://www.census.gov/prod/2003pubs/02statab/construct.pdf; "Historical Income Tables–Families," Housing and Household Economic Statistics Division, Bureau of the Census, U.S. Department of Commerce, revised July 8, 2004, Table F-3, available online at http://www.census.gov/hhes/income/histinc/f03.html.

14. For a survey, see Frank, *Luxury Fever,* Chapter 3.

15. Robert H. Frank, Bjornulf Ostvik-White, and Adam Levine, "Expenditure Cascades," mimeo, Cornell University, 2004.

16. The estimated coefficient for this variable was actually negative, though not statistically significant. Perhaps higher taxes in districts with high per pupil expenditures more than offset the positive effect of better schools.

17. Frank, Ostvik-White, and Levine, "Expenditure Cascades."

18. Samuel Bowles and Yongjin Park, "Emulation, Inequality, and Work Hours: Was Thorstein Veblen Right?" mimeo, Santa Fe Institute, 2002.

19. See, for example, James J. Choi et al., "For Better or for Worse: Default Effects and 401(k) Savings Behavior," NBER Working Paper no. w8651, National Bureau of Economic Research, Cambridge, Mass., December 2001, available online at http://papers.nber.org/papers/w8651.pdf. Also see Richard H. Thaler and Shlomo Benartzi, "Save More Tomorrow: Using Behavioral Economics to Increase Employee Saving," *Journal of Political Economy* 112, no. S1 (February 2004): S164–87.

20. See Robert E. Hall and Alvin Rabushka, *The Flat Tax,* 2nd ed. (Stanford, Calif.: Hoover Institution Press, 1995), for a discussion of the so-called flat tax, a form of consumption tax. For earlier proposals of a progressive consumption tax, see Irving Fisher and Herbert W. Fisher, *Constructive Income Taxation* (New York: Harper and Brothers, 1942); David F. Bradford, "The Case for a Personal Consumption Tax," in Joseph A. Pechman, ed., *What Should Be Taxed: Income or Expenditure?* (Washington, D.C.: Brookings Institution, 1980), pp. 75–113; Paul N. Courant and Edward M. Gramlich, "The Expenditure Tax: Has the Idea's Time Finally Come?" in Walter Heller, ed., *Tax Policy: New Directions and Possibilities* (Washington, D.C.: Center for National Policy, 1984); Laurence S. Seidman, *The USA Tax: A Progressive Consumption Tax* (Cambridge, Mass.: MIT Press, 1997).

21. Jack Hirshleifer, "Purchase Disorder" (review of Frank, *Luxury Fever*) *Reason,* June 1999, available online at http://reason.com/9906/bk.jh.purchase .shtml.

CHAPTER 5

1. There are four occupational systems: for blue-collar workers in the private sector, for white-collar workers in the private sector, for local government workers, and for central government workers.

2. *Ageing and Income: Financial Resources and Retirement in Nine OECD Countries,* Organization for Economic Cooperation and Development, Paris, 2001, p. 68.

3. On the basis of the intermediate assumptions, with real wage growth of 1.1 percent. See *The 2003 Annual Report of the Board of Trustees of the Federal Old-Age and Survivors Insurance and the Disability Insurance Trust Funds,* Social Security Administration, March 17, 2003, pp. 3, 6, available online at http://www.ssa.gov/OACT/TR/TR03/tr03.pdf.

4. Edward Palmer, "Swedish Pension Reform: Its Past and Its Future" in Martin Feldstein and Horst Siebert, eds., *Social Security Pension Reform in Europe* (Chicago: University of Chicago Press, 2002), pp. 171–205.

5. Although the labor market parties were not included in the group, a "reference group" consisting of the unions was continuously briefed on the progress of the group.

6. Ann-Charlotte Ståhlberg, *Pensionssystemets Inverkan på Hushållens Sparande* [The Effect of the Pension System on Savings] (Stockholm: Allmänna Förlaget, 1988).

7. Palmer, "Swedish Pension Reform."

8. Since the Swedish reform, several other countries have introduced NDC systems, including Italy, Poland, and Latvia. See ibid.

9. After the reform, earnings-related old-age benefits were separated from other kinds of social insurance programs: programs such as disability insurance that had previously been a part of the pension system were transferred outside. The calculations of disability benefits were changed and linked more closely with the system for sickness benefits.

10. Ministry of Health and Social Affairs, Sweden, *Reformerat Pensionssystem* [A Reformed Pension System] (Stockholm: Allmänna Förlaget, 1994), pp. 353–83.

11. "Conventional defined contribution system" means a funded defined contribution system with individual accounts.

12. Provisions for survivor benefits are made outside of the pension system and are temporary.

13. The introduction of individual accounts will increase private saving only if it constitutes new saving. It is likely that there will be an offset between pensions and nonpension savings. For an overview, see William Gale, "The Impact of Pensions and 401(k) Plans on Saving: A Critical Assessment of the State of the Literature," paper prepared for a conference entitled "ERISA after 25 Years: A Framework for Evaluating Pension Reform," National Press Club, Washington, D.C., September 17, 1999, available online at http://www.brookings.edu/dybdocroot/es/events/erisa/99papers/erisa4.pdf.

14. The carve-out was the result of an agreement not to decrease the scale of the public system.

15. Contributions to the funded pillar are invested in low-risk government bonds until individual pension rights have been established. This occurs when employer and employee tax statements have been consolidated, which takes an average of eighteen months.

16. Funds that wish to participate must sign a contract with the PPM. The contract governs the fee structure for the fund and reporting requirements. Funds can charge the same fees for participants in the pension system as they would in the private market. But since most of the administration of the accounts is undertaken by PPM, the actual cost for the fund managers

should be lower than in the private market. Therefore, funds have to rebate the PPM a share of the fees, and the PPM then passes on the savings to participants. The size of the rebate is determined by a complex formula and is determined by the fees the fund charges and the size of the fund; popular funds and high-cost funds have to pay a larger rebate.

17. Following the pension reform, three of the four occupational systems also introduced individual accounts in their plans. The contribution rates in these systems vary between 2.5 and 4 percent, which means that workers in Sweden contribute between 5 and 6.5 percent to individual accounts.

18. The transition period was originally twenty years but was shortened because the reform was delayed.

19. Although individuals born in the late 1940s and early 1950s will get 50 percent or more of their pension benefits from the new system, these cohorts have already been in the work force for twenty years or more. Many of their decisions about labor supply and savings were made under the old system. In part for this reason, the pension rights earned in the old system until 1994 are guaranteed for the transitional cohorts in the event that their benefits in the reformed system are lower.

20. Currently, the buffer funds amount to about three times the annual benefit payments.

21. The Swedish Pension System Annual Report 2002, National Social Insurance Board, Sweden, Stockholm, 2002, p. 9, English-language version available online at http://www.rfv.se/english/pdf/arsred02e.pdf.

22. The calculation of the balance ratio involves only current values, and no projections are made for assets and liabilities. Traditional projections of the financial status of the pension system are presented in the Technical Appendix to the *Swedish Pension System Annual Report 2002*.

CHAPTER 6

1. *Report of the 1994–1996 Advisory Council on Social Security,* Social Security Administration, 1997, available online at http://www.ssa.gov/policy/adcouncil/toc.htm.

2. Michael J. Graetz and Jerry L. Mashaw, *True Security: Rethinking American Social Insurance* (New Haven: Yale University Press, 2000).

3. Dallas Salisbury, ed., *The Future of Private Retirement Plans* (Washington, D.C.: Employee Benefit Research Institute, 2000).

4. *The 2004 Annual Report of the Board of Trustees of the Federal Old-Age and Survivors Insurance and the Disability Insurance Trust Funds,*

Social Security Administration, March 23, 2004, available online at http://www.ssa.gov/OACT/TR/TR04/tr04.pdf.

5. Congressional Budget Office, "The Long-Term Budget Outlook," December 2003, available online at http://www.cbo.gov/showdoc.cfm?index=4916&sequence=0.

6. President Clinton, speech at the Concord Coalition/AARP Social Security Forum (town hall meeting, University of New Mexico, Albuquerque, July 27, 1998).

7. Henry J. Aaron, testimony before the Senate Committee on the Budget, January 19, 1999, p. 3.

8. Congressional Budget Office, "Long-Term Budget Outlook."

CHAPTER 7

1. An alternative indexing method that would have caused real benefits to rise more slowly than real wages was proposed by some members of the Senate Finance Committee, but it was rejected by Congress as a whole. After retirement, Social Security benefits are adjusted for price increases rather than wage increases, but this affects the time path of benefits during retirement rather than the relationship between wage growth rates and the growth rate of benefit entitlements.

2. Lawrence H. Thompson, "The Social Security Reform Debate," *Journal of Economic Literature* 21, no. 4 (December 1983): 1425–67.

3. The trustees calculate that by 2030 the combination of SMI premiums and copays will amount to 19 percent of the average Social Security benefit. The estimates shown here are lower because the benefit for an illustrative average earner is some 25 percent higher than the actual average Social Security benefit. See *The 2003 Annual Report of the Board of Trustees of the Federal Hospital Insurance and Federal Supplementary Medical Insurance Trust Funds,* March 17, 2003, Table II.C14, available online at http://www.cms.hhs.gov/publications/trusteesreport/2003/tr.pdf.

4. Stephanie Maxwell, Marilyn Moon, and Misha Segal, "Growth in Medicare and Out-of-Pocket Spending: Impact on Vulnerable Beneficiaries," report, Commonwealth Fund, New York, January 2001, pp. 10–32, available online at http://www.cmwf.org/usr_doc/maxwell_increases_430.pdf. The adjustments to these numbers are discussed in the explanation of the calculations.

5. Mark Lino, "Expenditures on Children by Families" (Miscellaneous Publication no. 1528-1998), *1998 Annual Report,* Center for Nutrition Policy and Promotion, U.S. Department of Agriculture, 1999, p. 15, available

online at http://www.usda.gov/cnpp/crc98.PDF. Lino's estimates are broken into six age groups. For the average-income household they range from $8,240 for children under three to $9,340 for children ages fifteen to seventeen. For the high-income household they range from $12,260 for children under age three to $13,510 for those ages fifteen to seventeen. These estimates are for a married couple with two children.

INDEX

Aaron, Henry, 104
AARP, 40
Adverse selection, 62, 89
Affluent families. *See* High-income
  families
Age at retirement. *See* Retirement
  age
Age discrimination, 38, 40, 44
Aged. *See* Older workers
Ainslie, George, 48
Annuities, 74, 76–78, 95, 121
ATP (Allmän Tjänstepension).
  See Earnings-related
  benefit (Sweden)

Baby boomers, 2, 3, 9, 34–35,
  115, 116; retirement income
  of, 41, 76, 124
Blue-collar jobs, 31, 38, 40, 133n1
Bowles, Samuel, 57
Bridge jobs, 34
Buffer funds (Sweden), 75–76, 77,
  78
Businesses. *See* Employers and
  pension plans

Canada, 67–68
Cato Institute, 99, 101, 104–5
CBO. *See* Congressional Budget
  Office

Choi, James J., 58
Clinton, Bill, 104
Collective responsibility, 7, 84, 97,
  99. *See also* Intergenerational
  equity; Social contract
College-educated workers. *See*
  Education, and jobs
Congressional Budget Office
  (CBO), 35, 103, 106
Consumer debt, 48, 54–55, 95
Consumer Expenditure Survey, 122
Consumption, 49, 50–57, 122;
  effect on savings, 58–59, 64
Consumption tax, 60–63, 64
Cost of living, 16–17, 22–23,
  50–57
Cross-generational social insur-
  ance. *See* Intergenerational
  transfers
Cutler, David, 11–12

Debt. *See* Consumer debt
Deficits. *See* Social Security,
  deficits
Defined benefit plans, vii, 18–19,
  20, 21–22, 24, 30, 45, 65, 113
Defined contribution plans, vii, 1,
  18, 22, 24, 113; definition,
  19–20, 134n11; for health
  insurance, 108

Note: Page numbers followed by letters *n* and *t* refer to notes and tables,
respectively.

About the Contributors

ROBERT H. FRANK is the Henrietta Johnson Louis Professor of Management and professor of economics at Cornell's Johnson Graduate School of Management. His books, which include *Choosing the Right Pond; Passions within Reason; Microeconomics and Behavior; Principles of Economics* (with Ben Bernanke); *Luxury Fever;* and *What Price the Moral High Ground?*, have been translated into nine languages. *The Winner-Take-All Society,* coauthored with Philip Cook, received a Critic's Choice Award, was named a Notable Book of the Year by the *New York Times,* and was included in *BusinessWeek*'s list of the ten best books of 1995.

TERESA GHILARDUCCI is associate professor of economics at the University of Notre Dame. She is a member of the American Economics Association and the Industrial Relations Research Association. She has received many awards and honors, including the Industrial Relations Research Association Dissertation Roundtable Award and the Mary Ingraham Bunting Institute Fellowship. She is the author of *Labor's Capital: The Economics and Politics of Private Pensions* and coauthor of *Portable Pensions for Casual Labor Markets.* She has been a member of the National Academy of Social Insurance since 1994.

CATHERINE HILL is the research associate at the American Association of University Women Educational Foundation. Prior to taking this position in 2004, she was director of income security policy at the National Academy of Social Insurance, working on projects on health and income security for an aging workforce and on Social Security. She served as study director for the Social Security Project at the Institute for Women's Policy Research. In this role, she directed the Institute's research on economic issues facing older women with particular attention to Social Security and federal pension policy.

JOHN H. LANGBEIN is Sterling Professor of Law and Legal History at Yale Law School. He teaches and writes in four fields: trust and estate law, pension and employee benefit law, Anglo-American and European legal history, and modern comparative law. He has written extensively in the leading law reviews about pension, investment, probate, and trust law. He is a member of the American Academy of Arts and Sciences.

MAYA C. MACGUINEAS is the executive director of the Committee for a Responsible Federal Budget and the codirector of the Retirement Security Program at the New America Foundation. She has more than a decade of experience on issues related to the budget, entitlements, and taxes. Previously, she served as a Social Security adviser to the McCain presidential campaign and has worked at the Brookings Institution, the Concord Coalition, and on Wall Street. She currently serves on the National Governing Boards of Third Millennium, Common Cause, My Sister's Place, and Centrists.org.

JERRY L. MASHAW is Sterling Professor of Law and a professor at the Institute of Social and Policy Studies at Yale University. He is a widely published expert on subjects concerning administrative law, legislation, federal health and safety regulation, and social welfare policy. He has written many books, the most recent being *True Security: Rethinking American Social Insurance,* with coauthor Michael Graetz. He is a founding member and the current president of the National Academy of Social Insurance and chaired its 1996 study on *Balancing Security and Opportunity: The Challenge of Disability Income Policy.*

WILLIAM A. NISKANEN, an economist, has been chairman of the Cato Institute since 1985. His previous positions include service as a member and acting chairman of the Council of Economic Advisers and director of economics at the Ford Motor Company. His professional specialities, as illustrated in the title of one of his five books, have been *Policy Analysis and Public Choice.*

VAN DOORN OOMS is senior fellow and formerly senior vice president and director of research of the Committee for Economic Development. He was executive director for policy and chief economist of the Committee on the Budget, U.S. House of Representatives, from 1989 to 1991 and was the Budget Committee's chief economist during 1981–88. A member of the National Academy of Social Insurance since 2003, he taught economics at Yale University and at Swarthmore College before coming to Washington.

JOHN L. PALMER has been a professor of economics and public administration and past dean of the Maxwell School of Citizenship and Public Affairs at Syracuse University since 1988. Previously, he was a senior fellow at the Urban Institute and at the Brookings Institution and an adjunct professor at the Kennedy School of Government at Harvard. He was assistant secretary for planning and evaluation in the U.S. Department of Health and Human Services from 1979 to 1981. In late 2000, he was appointed to a four-year term as public trustee for Medicare and Social Security. A founding member of the National Academy of Social Insurance and president from 1997 to 1999, he now serves on its Board of Directors.

JOSEPH F. QUINN is dean of the College of Arts and Sciences and professor of economics at Boston College. He also has been a visiting professor at the University of New South Wales in Sydney, Australia, the Graduate School of Public Policy at the University of California, Berkeley, and the Institute for Research on Poverty at the University of Wisconsin–Madison. He has written on the economics of aging, the determinants of the individual retirement decision, recent trends in the work and retirement patterns of older Americans, and Social Security reform. He is a founding member of the National Academy of Social Insurance and now serves on its Board of Directors.

VIRGINIA P. RENO is a founding member and vice president for income security policy at the National Academy of Social Insurance. She is currently directing the study *Uncharted Waters: Paying Benefits from Individual Savings Accounts in Federal Retirement Policy.* Past studies she has directed include: *Health and Income Security for an Aging Workforce; Evaluating Issues in Privatizing Social Security;* and *Balancing Security and Opportunity: The Challenge of Disability Income Policy.* She has held research and policy positions at the U.S. Social Security Administration.

ANNIKA SUNDÉN is a research associate at the Center for Retirement Research at Boston College and a senior economist with the Swedish National Social Insurance Board. Previously, she was an economist in the Division of Research and Statistics at the Federal Reserve Board.

Her recent publications include *Portfolio Choice, Trading and Returns in a Large 401(k) Plan; Coming Up Short: The Challenge of 401(k) Plans;* and *How Will Sweden's New Pension System Work?* She has been a member of the National Academy of Social Insurance since 2001.

LAWRENCE H. THOMPSON is a senior fellow at the Urban Institute. His current work focuses on the future of the U.S. public pension system and on improving pension administration around the world. He serves as a consultant to the World Bank, the Asian Development Bank, and the International Labor Office and has been working most recently in Russia, Azerbaijan, and China. He was principal deputy commissioner of the U.S. Social Security Administration. Previous to that, he was assistant comptroller general and chief economist of the U.S. General Accounting Office. A founding member of the National Academy of Social Insurance, he has served as its president and on its Board of Directors.